QUESTIONS

by Stacia McKeever

illustrated by Dan Lietha

Answers in Genesis®

PO Box 510 • Hebron, KY 41048 • USA
www.AnwersInGenesis.org

First printing: Januray 2007

ISBN: 978-1-60092-028-4

Cover design: Dan Lietha
Interior layout: Diane King
Cd design: Daniel Lewis
Editors: Lori Jaworski and Becky Stelzer

Scientific content checked by: Bodie Hodge, Dr. Jason Lisle, Dr. David Menton, Dr. Terry Mortenson, Dr. Georgia Purdom, Michael Oard, Roger Patterson

Printed in the United States of America

Table of Contents

About the Authors

Stacia McKeever graduated *summa cum laude* in biology and psychology from Clearwater Christian College in 1997. She has worked full-time for *Answers in Genesis*–USA since then, and coauthored the "Answers for Kids" section in *Creation* magazine for several years. Stacia has written articles for *Creation* magazine, *Teach Kids!*, and the AiG website, and has led workshops centered on the "Seven C's of History" for children at AiG seminars. She lives with her husband, Seth, in the Greater Cincinnati Area.

Dan Lietha has been drawing since he was a child. He graduated in 1987 from the Joe Kubert School of Cartoon and Graphic Art and has been a full-time professional cartoonist since 1991. Since joining the *Answers in Genesis* staff in 1997, he has illustrated several books (including *A is for Adam, When Dragons' Hearts Were Good,* and *The Great Dinosaur Mystery Solved!*), created comic strips for the AiG newsletter and website, and produced countless illustrations which the AiG speakers use to effectively communicate the message that God's Word can be trusted from the beginning. Dan, his wife Marcia, and their daughter Hannah currently reside in the Greater Cincinnati Area.

Dear Teacher,

The *Questions* curriculum is designed to be used by itself or in conjunction with other curricula in the *Answers For Kids* series. There will be some overlap of the information presented in the different curricula. We suggest presenting *Beginnings,* followed by *The Seven C's of History*, followed by *Questions.*

Lesson Components

1. Lesson: We trust these lessons will help you to teach children to uphold the Bible's authority and to answer the questions that are hurled at them by today's increasingly evolutionized culture. In various places throughout the lessons, we suggest having children read a verse or paragraph out loud. Please feel free to modify this idea according to the abilities of your students or your constraints as a teacher. Please note that we have changed the format of the lessons. ILLUSTRATIONS are marked as such. **Bolded** sentences are notes to the teacher. Non-bolded sentences are to be read to students.
2. Activity ideas: This section provides suggested ideas for activities for you to incorporate into the lessons, as you have time.
3. Extension Activities: For those interested in using *Questions* as a spring-board to discussing other topics, we have provided additional study ideas.
4. Recommended resources: This section provides a list of materials that supplement the topic being discussed.
5. CD-ROM: The accompanying CD-ROM contains the illustrations and handouts that will be used throughout this curriculum. You may wish to use the illustrations in a digital presentation (such as PowerPoint), or simply print them out on transparencies or on plain paper. The CD-ROM also contains songs and words to the songs.

continued next page

6. Student handouts: You will need one set of student handouts per child in your class (there are seven handouts per set—these are not included on the CD-ROM). We have included one complete set with the Teacher's Manual—additional sets are available from www.answersbookstore.com.

Verse review ideas

Each lesson contains a suggested memory verse. We have listed just a few of the many ways to help the students learn the scripture passages.

- Write the verse on a chalk or white board. Have students repeat it together. Erase a word and repeat it again. Continue to do this until you've erased the entire verse.
- Make a song out of the verse—make up your own tune, or use the tune of a familiar song.
- Write each word of the verse on an index card and have children put the cards in order (if you have a large class, you may want to make several sets of the verse).
- Ask for volunteers to say the verse without looking at it—have the other students follow along and help the volunteer when he needs it.

Scripture reading ideas

This curriculum is based heavily around reading passages from the Bible. There are several ways you might do this (depending on your constraints as a teacher, etc.):

- Choose one student to read the entire verse assignment.
- Choose one student to begin reading, and have each student read a verse or two in turn.
- Assign parts to students, e.g., narrator, Adam, Eve.
- Read the passage while students follow along.
- Have students read the passage silently.

We trust this curriculum will be a blessing and encouragement to you and those in your class. If you have any questions or comments, please email me at smckeever@answersingenesis.org.

Sincerely,
Stacia McKeever

LESSON

1

Where did humans come from?

Memory verse: Psalm 139:14
Materials:

From CD:

- Illustrations 1-00–1-18
- Handouts L1a, L1b, L1c
- Song *I Don't Believe in Evolution*

Overview

Either overtly in school or subtly through cartoons and movies, children are taught fairly early that we are related to animals and share a common ancestor with apes. As adults, we often hear in the popular press of a new find that "proves" we came from an ape-like creature. However, the truth is that humans were created by God separately from animals and in His image. This lesson explores the biblical and scientific answers to the question "where did humans come from?" It helps children learn to think critically about secular claims about our past.

ILLUSTRATION 1-00. **Welcome students to class, etc.**

How many of you have ever seen the movies *Ice Age* or *Dinosaur*? **Allow children to respond.**

As much as we may enjoy watching movies and television programs such as these, we need to be aware that they are not telling us the truth about what happened in the past.

ILLUSTRATION 1-01. Over the next few weeks we'll be learning the true history of the universe that God has revealed to us in the Bible. As we learn about what the Bible and science teach us, we'll find out how to answer many questions that people ask about the past: Where did we come from? What about the dinosaurs? Why do we look so different from each other?

Let's start this lesson by thinking about what we've heard about where we come from. Have you ever heard that we share an ancestor with apes and monkeys, or that millions of years ago apemen wandered the earth? Maybe someone has told you that you're just another animal. **Allow children to respond. They may have read something in a textbook or seen something on television or in a movie.**

In this lesson, we're going to learn what the Bible teaches about where we came from and how we can respond when we hear claims like these.

ILLUSTRATION 1-02. First, let's take a look at this picture. How many of you see an old woman in this picture? **Wait for answers.** And how many of you see a young woman? **Wait for answers. Then point out the old woman and young woman, for those who couldn't see them.**

There are two different ways to view this picture, aren't there? It's the same picture, but depending on how you look at it, you can see something different.

The world around us is like that, too. For example, two people can look at the same fossil and come to completely different conclusions about what it means. **Note: a fossil is any evidence of past life found in a rock.**

This happens because people have different ideas of why the world is the way it is. They believe different things about what happened in the past. There are two main ideas about the history of our universe.

ILLUSTRATION 1-03. The first idea comes from the collection of 66 books that we call the Bible. Who wrote the Bible? **Wait for answers. God used over 40 different men to write down what He wanted them to record.**

ILLUSTRATION 1-04. **Briefly explain the biblical timeline of history:**

Creation: God created all things in six actual days around 6,000 years ago. Everything was very good.

Corruption: Adam disobeyed, and his disobedience changed the entire world.

Catastrophe: God sent a globe-covering Flood as a judgment for the sin of mankind.

Confusion: God confused the people's languages at Babel, causing the various family groups to go their separate ways.

Christ: God sent His Son, Jesus Christ, to earth to become a human so that He could live a perfect life in obedience to the Father.

Cross: Jesus died on the Cross for the sin of mankind.

Consummation: One day all things will be "very good" again for those who have received the free gift of eternal life.

ILLUSTRATION 1-05. Those who accept this view use the Bible to help them make sense of the world around them.

ILLUSTRATION 1-06. The other idea comes from those who don't believe the Bible. This view says that the universe came into being on its own, and that countless millions of years ago a single-celled creature appeared on earth. This was supposedly our first ancestor, which we share with all living things. Over the years, this creature's descendants gradually changed into the wide variety of animals and plants that we see today. Eventually, humans came from an ape-like creature.

ILLUSTRATION 1-07. Those who accept this view use evolutionary ideas to help them make sense of the world around them.

That's a quick summary of the two main ideas about the past. They're very different, aren't they? How do we know which view is the correct one? **Allow children to respond.**

It would be helpful if someone who witnessed, or who was involved in, past events recorded what happened, wouldn't it?

Do you know anyone who has been around from the beginning, and whom you would trust to tell you the truth? **Wait for answers.** Correct—God! God is eternal, which means He doesn't have a beginning or end. He has always existed. And God always tells the truth. So we can trust His account of history to be completely accurate.

Where has God recorded His account of history? **Wait for answers.** Right—in the Bible! So, in order to learn about why the world is the way it is, we need to study the Bible.

Let's take a closer look at how the Bible answers our question for today, "Where did we come from?"

Read Genesis 1:24–31; 2:4–7, 18–24 together.

ILLUSTRATION 1-08. The Bible teaches that humans were made in whose image? **We were created in the image of God. We were made in the image of the holy, eternal, Creator God, not in the image of ape-like creatures.**

How did God make the animals? **He spoke, and the land produced living creatures according to their kinds (Genesis 1:24–25).**

Compare that to how God made man. What is different? **Allow children to respond. Encourage them to see that God formed man directly from the dust and breathed into him the breath of life (Genesis 2:7), whereas He commanded the earth to bring forth the animals (Genesis 1:24). Note that the Bible teaches that Adam was a special creation of the Lord; Adam was not created from a pre-existing animal.**

Another difference between animals and humans is that Eve was created from Adam's side (Genesis 2:21–22). None of the female animals were created from the sides of the male animals. Also, God made humans in His image (Genesis 1:26)—He didn't do this for the animals. An additional point of difference between animals and humans is that, when Jesus came to earth, He came as a man, not an animal, and He died for men, not animals.

Read Psalm 100:3 together.

So what's the answer to today's question, "Where did humans come from?" **We were created by God in His image.**

ILLUSTRATION 1-09. Let's look at our verse for today, Psalm 139:14. **Have students read it together.**

ILLUSTRATION 1-10. The people who believe this evolutionary view of history believe we came from animals, and that we are just another type of animal. They believe that the many similarities between us and apes show that we were once apes. The Bible tells us that we were created in the image of God. We are not just another type of animal. We are fearfully and wonderfully made in the image of God.

ILLUSTRATION 1-11. It's true that there are some similarities. Let's look at some of them. **Discuss some similarities: two eyes, two ears, nose, mouth, teeth, hands with opposable thumbs (thumbs that help us grip an object), arms, legs, heart, stomach, eat some of the same foods, breathe, have backbones, give birth to live young.**

The Bible teaches that the same God created animals and humans, doesn't it? So, we might expect to find some of the same types of features among animals and humans. However, the Bible is also clear that God created us differently.

ILLUSTRATION 1-12. We've already looked at a few ways that the Bible teaches animals and humans are different. Let's look at a few more. Can you think of any other differences between apes and people? **Apes don't have a complex language system, don't drive cars, don't build computers, don't make or play musical instruments, and aren't creative. They don't go to church to learn about God, don't have friends over to play board games or watch a television program, don't have birthday parties or celebrate Christmas, can't have a relationship with God, don't choose which outfit to wear, don't go shopping for groceries or new shoes, etc. God gave humans dominion over the animals (Genesis 1:28).**

ILLUSTRATION 1-13. The people who believe this view of history also believe that they have found evidence that we have evolved from ape-like creatures over millions of years. They claim that they have found bones of supposed "apemen" that show how we've changed over the years.

ILLUSTRATION 1-14. They often use pictures like this to illustrate the evolution of man.

ILLUSTRATION 1-15. But we need to keep in mind that pictures like these are only an illusion. That means that they aren't real. They were drawn by somebody who didn't believe the Bible's account of history.

ILLUSTRATION 1-16. We also need to keep in mind that when people find bones, the bones don't come with attached tags that say, "Hi, I'm an apeman!" The bones need to be carefully studied to find out what type of creature they belonged to.

Let's take a look at some of the more famous so-called apemen, and find out the truth behind the illusions.

Pass out the "Where did humans come from?" student handout and read the "Looking a Little Closer" page together. You may also want to discuss how the movies mentioned above (*Ice Age, Dinosaur, Curious George,* or any other movie or television program) portray human ancestors and why this portrayal isn't correct. See www.answersingenesis.org/go/disney-dinosaur and www.answersingenesis.org/ice-age-movie for movie reviews.

Illustration 1-17. The Bible explains the truth about where humans came from, and we can trust it. When we hear something that doesn't agree with what the Bible teaches, we need to closely examine what was actually found. Sometimes, we may need to wait a few years to find out what type of bones they really are, but we can be certain that God's Word—which never changes—is true.

Review today's memory verse: Psalm 139:14.

Discussion Questions

1. On which day of the Creation Week did God create apes and monkeys?

   Answer: Day 6—the same day that God created humans.

2. What do the following Bible verses teach about our purpose on earth? Genesis 1:26; Micah 6:8; Ecclesiastes 12:13.

   Answer: We are to be careful stewards of the earth, its resources and the animals and plants. We are to act justly, love mercy, and walk humbly with God. We are to fear God and keep His commandments. Discuss some practical ways that you and your students can fulfill our God-given purpose on earth.

Activity Ideas

1. Take a trip to the zoo and visit the primate enclosure. Look for similarities and differences between the primates (monkeys, chimps, gorillas, etc.) and humans.

2. Print out L1a and L1b. Make copies for children to color.

3. Create a collage based on the similarities/differences section of the lesson.

Find pictures (in old magazines, for example) or draw pictures of apes and humans and other types of activities or ideas that accentuate the differences between us and animals. For example, picture of a chimp and a human next to a picture of an airplane—which one would fly the plane? Orangutan and human beside a computer—which one built it? Gorilla and human beside a store—which one goes shopping for clothes and food? Monkey and human beside a church—which one can have a relationship with God? Write across the top of your collage, "I am not just an animal—I was created in the image of God!"

Some people will point out that both apes and humans use tools (see www.answersingenesis.org/go/tools). However, only humans use tools to make tools! Additionally, animals throughout the world use tools. What examples of this can you find? Draw or cut out pictures of a variety of animals using tools. Add these to your collage.

Another difference between humans and apes or monkeys is the shape of our feet (see Illustration 1-18). Non-human primates have feet with opposable thumbs (digits used for grasping or climbing). On the collage (or on separate pieces of paper) make prints of each child's hands and feet, using finger paints. Have each child sign and date his prints.

4. Research the various so-called "missing links" listed below. What are they now known to be? What other alleged ancestors of humans have you heard about? What have these turned out to be? (For help, visit www.answersingenesis.org/go/anthropology, or read *Bones of Contention* by Marvin Lubenow, or *Skeletons in Your Closet* by Gary Parker.)

   Cro-Magnon man

   Piltdown man

   Nebraska man

   Australopithecus africanus

   Australopithecus afarensis

   Ardipithecus ramidus

   Homo habilis

   Homo erectus (Java man, Peking man)

   Ramapithecus

5. Read "The Evidence" page from the student handout. The point of this page is that sometimes something we see on television (or read in a book or magazine) might make us doubt whether the Bible is true. But later on, we find that what we were taught was wrong, and we shouldn't have doubted God's Word. Instead, we should have doubted what the people on television or in the book were saying.

6. Use a tangram to demonstrate the human ability to be creative (another aspect that separates us from animals). See *Science and the Bible*, volume 2, experiment 18 (or look up "tangram" on the internet). Print L1c and make a copy for each student. Cut the square into seven pieces along the lines. Challenge students to creatively use the pieces to construct different shapes (animals, flowers, letters, numbers, people, etc.), making sure the pieces touch, don't overlap, and lie flat. What else can you find out about how to make a tangram and its history? See also *Tangram Puzzles* (by Chris Crawford), and *Tangrams: 330 Puzzles* (by Ronald Read) for design ideas.

Extension Activities

History

Find out who may have been behind the famous Piltdown man hoax. Was it Charles Dawson, Sir Arthur Keith, Sir Arthur Conan Doyle, Martin A.C. Hinton, or someone else? Write a short essay detailing your findings.

There have been several other apemen hoaxes in the past. Find out more about the Minnesota Iceman hoax.

- www.answersingenesis.org/go/anthropology

Language Arts

The ability to speak and write using a complex grammatical system sets us apart from animals. One way that we can express ourselves through writing is poetry. Choose three different types of poetry to study. Have students write a poem in each style on the following topics: the differences between animals and humans, what it means to be created in the image of God, what it means to be fearfully and wonderfully made.

- www.shadowpoetry.com/resources/wip/poetry.html

Science

There have been some claims that animals have learned to talk. Read the articles at www.answersingenesis.org/go/linguistics.

Lesson 1

How does the human vocal tract differ from the vocal tract of most animals?

- www.phon.ox.ac.uk/~jcoleman/phonation.htm
- en.wikipedia.org/wiki/Larynx

Although animals and birds may not communicate as we do, they are able to communicate with others of their kind. Visit www.answersingenesis.org/go/design. Find out how the following communicate: honey bees, ruffled grouse, chameleons, ants. How do other animals communicate?

Bible

What does the Bible say about communication?

What does the Bible say about how we are to use our ability to communicate? Have children look up the following passages in a "Sword drill." (This is not an exhaustive list—please modify as necessary.) Have the children hold up their Bibles (closed), with one hand on each side of the Bible. Announce the verse, have children repeat it, and say, "Go!" The first child to find the verse stands and reads the verse when called on.

Psalm 16:8–10, 35:27–28, 37:30, 119:171–172, 150:6; Proverbs 4:24, 6:16–19, 10:11, 10:13, 10:19–21, 12:13–14, 12:18–19, 12:22, 13:3, 15:1–2, 15:23, 16:13, 16:23–24, 16:28, 17:27–28, 18:21, 20:19, 21:23, 24:26, 25:11, 26:18–26, 27:2; Ephesians 4:17–32; Colossians 3:1–17; James 3:3–12

How does God communicate with us? How are we to communicate with our Creator?

What does "in the image of God" mean?

Read Genesis 1:26–27. What does it mean to be "made in the image of God"? Visit www.answersingenesis.org/go/image-of-God.

Recommended Resources

- *Bones of Contention* by Marvin Lubenow
- *Skeletons in Your Closet* by Gary Parker
- *Puzzle of Ancient Man* by Don Chittick

Lesson 1

Every so often, we'll read in the newspaper, or hear on TV something like, "Skull find proves man and apes share a common ancestor." But is this really true?

Some background

There are two main (and very different) ideas about the history of our universe.

The first idea comes from the collection of 66 books we call the Bible. From it, we can learn that God created all things in six normal-length days only a few thousand years ago. He explains in Genesis that He created the first man and woman on the sixth day of that first week, along with the various kinds of land animals. (He made the air and water creatures on Day 5. The various kinds of plants were made on Day 3.) Those who accept this view use the Bible to help them make sense of the world around them.

The second belief is based on the idea that the universe came into being on its own. Countless millions of years ago, a single-celled creature appeared on earth. This was supposedly our first ancestor, which we share with all living things. Over the years, this creature's descendants gradually changed into the wide

variety of animals and plants that we see today. This view is known as "evolution."

Those who accept this view use evolutionary ideas to help them make sense of the world around them.

Which is right?

Is it possible to know for certain which view of the past is correct? After all, none of us were around "in the beginning!" It's impossible for us to know firsthand what happened, and when.

However, because the Bible is the written record of One who has always existed and who always tells the truth, we can trust it to be an accurate account of history.

What's the truth?

So, do headlines, like the one quoted on the previous page, tell the truth? No. The first man was created from the dust of the ground (Genesis 2:7). God created the first woman from his rib (Genesis 2:21–24). Both were made in the image of God (Genesis 1:27). We don't share a common ancestor with apes!

It's important to carefully check what was actually found when we hear claims like the one above. Many times, the supposed "proof" of evolution is based on only a few bone fragments. Or it turns out to be a type of monkey or ape, or even a true human. But it is never a "transition" between an ape and humans.

The "evidence" (bones, for example) doesn't prove evolution is true. Neither does it "prove" the Bible is true. Rather, we interpret the evidence based on our belief in either evolution or the Bible. When we come across claims that a fossil discovery "proves" evolution, we should look more closely at what was really found.

THE EVIDENCE

Thy word is true from the beginning: and every one of thy righteous judgments endureth for ever.
Psalm 119:160

Looking a Little Closer

Evolutionists claim that humans and apes share a common ancestor that lived millions of year ago.

They say they have uncovered the fossils of supposed "apemen." But the first apeman was described and drawn long before any bones were found. The drawing was based purely on the belief that things made themselves without God (evolution).

If evolution were true, there should be thousands of fossils showing the transition from apelike creatures to humans. However, the "missing links" turn out to be nothing more than bones of humans, or bones of some type of extinct ape. Even evolutionists themselves don't always agree on how the bones should be interpreted!

We can't go wrong if we trust in the Word of God, which never changes and never needs to be updated. It tells us that humans are not evolved animals, but were created in the image of God.

Let's take a look at some of the more famous apemen fossils, and find out what they really are.

Neanderthal man—Neandertal is German for Neander Valley. This is where bones of this supposed "missing link" were first found about 150 years ago. Scientists now realize that Neanderthals were humans. They were our relatives—descendants of Adam and Eve (through Noah).

Java man—He was first found in East Java over 100 years ago. Now that we have more of the bones, it is clear that his body was similar to ours. He walked just like we do. The same is true for Peking man, who was discovered in China during the 1920s and '30s. Both are now called *Homo erectus,* or "upright man." Recent evidence shows that modern-looking early humans had children by both Neanderthals and *Homo erectus*, showing that they are all fully human people groups.

"Lucy"—"Lucy" is among the more famous "missing links." Careful research on the skull, inner ear, and other bones shows that Lucy is very similar to a pygmy chimpanzee. She did not walk upright like humans. Instead, she used her knuckles, like gorillas and chimps.

LESSON

2

Why do we look different?

Memory verse: Acts 17:26
Materials:

From CD:

- Illustrations 2-00–2-19
- Handout L2a
- Song *We're One Blood*

Overview

Racism is a hot topic in our society. Are there really different races of people? Should we be divided because of the shade of our skin or the color of our eyes? According to the Bible, there is only one race of people: the human race. No matter what we look like, we are all children of Adam and Eve (and, more recently, Noah and his sons). In this lesson, children will learn how to biblically and scientifically explain that we are all related, and that we're really all the same: we're all sinners in need of a Savior.

Lesson 2

Illustration 2-00. **Welcome students to class, etc.**

In this series of lessons, we're learning how to answer some of the questions that people ask about Christianity and the Bible. In the last lesson, we learned that we were created in the image of God. We do not share an ancestor with apes and monkeys, and we are *not* just another type of animal.

Illustration 2-01. Today, we're going to learn the answer to another question. First, let me ask you a question. How many of you have ever sung the song, "Jesus Loves the Little Children"? **Allow children to discuss and sing the song briefly.** This song says that all the children of the world are "red, brown, yellow, black, and white" (or "red and yellow, black and white").

If we were all created in God's image, then why are there so many different skin colors? Some of us have tan skin. Others have darker skin. Some have blue eyes. Others have brown eyes. Some have dark-colored hair. Others have light-colored hair.

We're going to find out how to answer the question: Why do we seemingly look different?

Illustration 2-02. Let's begin by thinking about our skin. Our skin is our largest organ. It has many important functions. It works as a barrier between the outside world and our insides. It helps us to keep our body at a constant temperature. And it helps us to sense the world around us.

Illustration 2-03. While it might not seem like our skin does much except keep us covered, this covering limits water loss from our body. We would only survive a matter of hours without it! In fact, if we were to examine a section of our skin, we would find a lot going on. For example, we would find glands that produce sweat and oil, vessels that carry our blood, nerve endings that help us touch and feel, and places where our hair grows!

Illustration 2-04. We would also find thousands of cells, called "melanocytes," that produce a pigment called "melanin." Melanin is the pigment that helps give your skin some color. There are two forms of melanin. One is dark brownish, the other is reddish. These pigments produce our particular shade of skin color.

Scientists have found that, no matter what we look like, we all have the same amount of melanocytes in our bodies.

Illustration 2-05. Inside each melanocyte is a set of "instructions," called DNA **(deoxyribonucleic acid)** that tells the melanocyte, among other things, how much melanin to produce.

Lesson 2

Illustration 2-06. If the DNA in your body tells your melanocytes to make a lot of melanin, and your skin keeps a lot of the melanin that is made, then your skin will be very dark brown. If your instructions say "make a little melanin," and your skin looses some of the melanin that is made, then your skin will be very light brown. And there are many combinations in between, as we can see from this picture.

(Technical aside: Differences in the shade of skin may be based in part on how much pigment is produced, and in part on how much pigment is preserved in the skin after it is produced. Special "transport vehicles" called melanosomes carry the melanin from the melanocytes to other cells that are capable of dividing (stem cells), primarily in the lowest layer of the epidermis. In these cells, the pigment serves its function as it forms a little dark umbrella over each nucleus. This protects the epidermal cells from being damaged by sun light. In people with lighter shades of skin, much of the pigment covering the stem cells is lost after these cells divide and their daughter cells move up in the epidermis to form the surface dead layer— the stratum corneum.)

The sun can cause our melanocytes to produce more melanin. But only to a certain point. For example, the melanocytes of the fair-skinned girl on the end will never be able to produce as much melanin as those of the girl on the bottom row, no matter how long she stays out in the sun.

No one really has "red" or "yellow" or "black" skin. We all have the same basic color, just different shades of it. We all share the same pigment—our bodies just have more or less of it!

Illustration 2-07. Melanin also determines the color of your eyes. If you have a lot of it in the iris of your eyes, they will be brown. If you have a little melanin, your eyes will be blue. (The blue color in blue eyes is the result of the light scattering off the thin layer of brown-colored melanin.)

Illustration 2-08. What hair colors do you think result from a lot of melanin in our hair shafts? **Brown and black hair.** What hair color results from less melanin? **Blond hair.** Those with red hair lack the ability to produce much of the brownish form of melanin, so the reddish form is more evident.

Illustration 2-09. Our DNA also controls the basic shape of our eyes.

Illustration 2-10. Some people groups tend to have dark, curly hair with dark eyes and dark skin, while others have black, straight hair, dark almond-shaped eyes, and lighter skin, while still others have light hair, blue eyes, and very fair skin.

Where did our DNA come from in the first place, and why do people groups look so different?

Illustration 2-11. Let's remind ourselves of what the Bible teaches about our past.

Illustration 2-12. In the beginning, God created Adam. From the Bible, we learn that Adam was the very first man. **Read Genesis 2:7, and 1 Corinthians 15:45.** We also learn that Adam was alone—there was no one else like him. **Read Genesis 2:18–22 together.**

Illustration 2-13. Adam was alone until God created Eve from Adam's side. Eve was the very first woman—the Bible tells us that she was the mother of everyone. **Read Genesis 3:20.** God gave these first two people the best combination of DNA possible. Their skin was probably a "middle brown" shade.

Illustration 2-14. After they sinned and were sent from the Garden of Eden, Adam and Eve had many children. Some historians have suggested that they may have had over 50 children! Their children grew up, married each other, and had children of their own. The number of people (all children, grandchildren, great grandchildren ... of Adam and Eve) in the world continued to increase as time went on.

Note: This may bring up the question: If Adam and Eve were the only people in the world, who did their son Cain marry (Genesis 4:17)? The simple answer is that in the beginning, brothers and sisters married each other! For more information, visit www.answersingenesis.org/go/cains-wife.

Illustration 2-15. When God judged the wickedness of mankind with a globe-covering flood, He saved only Noah, his wife, his three sons, and their wives on the Ark. Everyone else died in the watery catastrophe—all of Noah's aunts, uncles, cousins, nephews, nieces, grandparents, etc. When the Flood was over, and the Ark had settled in the mountains of Ararat, Noah and his family were the only humans left on the whole entire earth. The Bible tells us that Noah's three sons were the fathers of all the people groups in the world. **Read Genesis 9:18–19.**

Illustration 2-16. Noah's descendants decided to build a tall tower with which they could worship the heavens. Why is this wrong? **Allow students**

to respond. The Creator is the only One who is worthy to receive worship; giving worship to anything other than the Lord God is a sin. Discuss some ways that people worship the heavens today (e.g., those who believe that life originated in outer space, those who look to the stars and planets for guidance). To encourage them to obey His command to fill the earth, God caused them to begin speaking different languages. **Read Genesis 11: 5–9.**

ILLUSTRATION 2-17. Because the family groups spoke different languages, they were unable to understand each other. They couldn't work together any more. They stopped working on the tower, and many family groups packed up their belongings and left the area.

ILLUSTRATION 2-18. They began to move to different parts of the world. Some of Ham's grandchildren started toward Africa, while others started moving toward Asia, eventually reaching the Americas. The families in Japheth's clan went toward Europe and India. And many in Shem's clan stayed in the areas of the Middle East. **For more information on this, see www.answersingenesis.org/go/grandsons.**

As they went, each of these groups took with it its own special set of characteristics (for instance, lighter skin and eye color, or darker skin and eye color). These characteristics were passed through the people's DNA to their children, and so on. Because the groups no longer freely mixed with other groups, the characteristics of each group became more and more prominent as new generations of children were born.

If we were to travel back in time to Babel and mix up the people into completely different family groups, people groups with completely different characteristics might result. For instance, we might find a fair-skinned group with tight, curly dark hair that has blue, almond-shaped eyes, or a group with very dark skin, blue eyes, and straight, brown hair! **Technical note: this is given as a general illustration that assumes each characteristic is independently inherited, although in some cases this may not be the case.**

ILLUSTRATION 2-19. Although we may hear about many different "races" of people, there is really only one race—the human race. Even though we may look very different and speak very different languages, we are actually all part of the same family. Noah was the great, great, great, great, great, great, great, great, etc., grandfather of us all!

In fact, because they are all descendants of Noah, most people groups have stories that are similar to the true accounts given in the Bible about Creation and the great Flood.

You may want to summarize the following legend, depending on the time you have available.

For instance, the Choctaw Indians of North America have passed this legend down through the years:

In ancient times after men had lived a long period upon the earth, they became very corrupt and wicked. They deluged the earth with so much blood and carnage that the Great Spirit finally decided to utterly destroy them. He, therefore, sent a prophet among them, who went from tribe to tribe and from village to village proclaiming the fearful tidings that the race was soon to be destroyed. No one paid any attention to him, however, and people went on in their wickedness as carelessly as ever. But one year, with the coming of autumn, mists and clouds gathered over the earth, so that there was no sun shining by day nor did the moon and stars light up the gloom of night.

One day, very suddenly, there came a crash of thunder much louder than had ever been heard before. The whole earth seemed to shake and tremble with the reverberation. Then, as people looked toward the north, they seemed to see a light—the first they had seen for many a long dark day. But whatever hope may have been aroused in their breasts was dissipated. For what they saw was not the return of the long lost sun, but it was the gleam of a great mountain of water, advancing in great billows from the north, covering the entire earth, and destroying everything in its path. With the cry, "Oka Falamah, Oka Falamah" (the returning waters, the returning waters), the doomed people turned away in one last vain effort to escape. But there was no escape. The whole earth was soon covered even to the tops of the mountains by the vast flood, and men and animals alike perished, leaving only a desolate wilderness of waters.

Of all mankind, only one remained, and that was the mysterious prophet who had so faithfully, yet vainly, proclaimed the warnings of the Great Spirit. This prophet had been directed by the Great Spirit to build a raft of sassafras logs, upon which he floated safely above the destroying flood, while he gazed sadly upon the dead bodies of men and beasts as they floated past him in the dark waters.

The prophet floated aimlessly about for many weeks, until at last one day he saw a large black bird circling over his raft. He cried to it for help, but the bird only uttered a few harsh croaks and flew away to be seen no more. Some days later the prophet saw a smaller bird, bluish in color, with red beak and eyes, hovering over the raft. Again he asked this bird if there was a spot of dry land to be found anywhere in the waste of waters. It hovered over him for a few moments, as if trying in its soft mournful voice to give the desired information, and then flew off toward the west where the new sun was again setting in splendor. Almost at once a strong wind arose which carried the raft in the direction in which the bird had gone. All night, it floated on under the moon and stars which shone again with renewed brightness.

When the sun rose the next morning, the prophet saw in the distance an island toward which his raft seemed to be drifting. Before the sun went down again, the raft had moved along until it touched the island, and the tired prophet landed. Glad to be on the earth once more, he lay down and slept until the sun rose the next day. Much refreshed, he then began to look about the island, where to his surprise, he found every variety of animal formerly found on the earth (except the mammoth), and all the birds and fowl also.

The prophet lived on this island for many days, until finally the waters passed away. The earth once more took its former appearance, with hills, valleys, and grassy prairies. But the Indian people never again became so rashly disobedient to the Great Spirit and never forgot the lesson of Oka Falamah, the "Returning Waters."

(This legend, which pre-dated the coming of missionaries to the Choctaw, was recorded by W.B. Morrison, and is available at www.tc.umn.edu/~mboucher/mikebouchweb/choctaw/flood1.htm.)

Briefly discuss some of the similarities and differences between this legend and the true account in Genesis: the reason for the flood, the prophet, how the prophet was saved, the role of birds, the activity of the winds, etc.

There are over 500 different accounts like this from people groups around the world. This shows us that as the grandchildren of Noah moved away they took with them the accounts of creation and the Flood that had been told to them by their fathers—Shem, Ham, and Japheth. Over time, the stories have changed, but God has given us His Word so that we can know the truth.

As we've seen, the differences between us aren't all that great! We are actually all part of one big family. And because we are all descendants of Adam, we have all inherited his sinful nature. All of us, no matter what skin shade or eye shape, are sinners (Romans 3:23). We all need to be saved from our sin so that we can spend eternity with our Creator. Jesus Christ paid the penalty for sin by dying on a cross and raising again three days later (1 Corinthians 15:1–4). Everyone who believes this, no matter where he lives, what people group he belongs to, or what he looks like, receives the free gift of eternal life (John 3:16–18).

Review the memory verse for this lesson: Acts 17:26.

Discussion Questions

1. Imagine if the children in your class suddenly spoke a different language, and the only people you could understand were those in your family (brothers, sisters, parents). How would you feel? What would you do?

   Answer: Allow for various responses.

2. Does the DNA that you have received from your parents tell your melanocytes to produce a lot of melanin, or a little melanin, or somewhere in between? What about the DNA in your irises? What does the DNA of your brothers and sisters tell their melanocytes to do?

   Answer: Allow for various responses. Continue to reinforce the idea that, no matter what our skin shade or eye color, we are all relatives, descendants of Adam and Eve, and all in the same boat—sinners in need of a Savior. You may want to use the science experiments in *Science and the Bible* on loving others (volume 1, number 17), or the importance of each member of the body of Christ (volume 2, number 22) to demonstrate these truths.

3. Even though we may look very different from each other, we all have one thing in common. Every person has sinned, and is need of hearing about salvation through Jesus Christ. Every tribe and nation needs to hear the good news of salvation. What are some ways that we can help to spread the good news?

   Answer: Allow for various responses: pray for missionaries, monetarily (or in other ways) support missionaries, go on missions trips (when older), share the good news with friends and neighbors, etc.

Activity Ideas

1. Print one copy of L2a for each child. Look through a crayon box to find a "middle brown." Use this to color Adam and Eve. Use other shades of brown to color their children to illustrate the variety within humans. What other colors represent colors within the human race? What colors are *not* shades of the human race?

2. Read through today's handout together.

3. Where did Noah's grandsons go? Read "The Sixteen Grandsons of Noah" (www.answersingenesis.org/go/grandsons), and place the name of each grandson on a world map on the area that he helped to populate after the split at Babel.

Extension Activities

History

Throughout history, some people have thought that those with certain skin shades are better than other people with a different skin shade or appearance. Find out about how the Australian Aborigines have been wrongly treated in centuries past. What is "apartheid"? Which people groups have been affected by apartheid? Why is apartheid wrong?

- www.answersingenesis.org/go/racism

Language Arts

Research the flood and creation myths and legends of other cultures. Write a summary of each legend. Compile the summaries in a three-ring binder, under "Creation Legends" or "Flood Legends." Use colored markers to highlight similarities between the legends (e.g., use yellow to highlight the reason for the flood, pink to highlight descriptions of the boat).

- www.answersingenesis.org/go/legends

Science

The DNA carries much more information about us than merely our skin shade or eye color. It also carries the information for how tall we can grow, what our nose will look like, how long our arms will be, how our ears will be shaped. Find out more about the information-storage capacity of DNA. If you were to write the information stored on one strand of our DNA, how many books would you fill? If you unraveled a strand of DNA in just one cell of your body, how long would it be? If you unraveled all the DNA in your body, how long would it be? What else can you find out about the marvelous DNA molecule?

- www.answersingenesis.org/go/warriors
- www.answersingenesis.org/go/basket
- www.answersingenesis.org/go/living-computer

- www.answersingenesis.org/go/message-molecule

Bible

What does the Bible teach about "interracial" marriage?

Read Genesis 2:19–24 and Matthew 19:1–6. What do these passages teach about the nature and origin of the doctrine of marriage?

(Marriage is to be between one man and one woman for life. Eve was made to be Adam's helper and companion for the rest of their lives. This is why we get married today—and why we stay married. This is also why men are not to marry other men (or many women) and women are not to marry other women.)

When you get older, it may be that the Lord will lead you to be married. What do the following passages teach about they type of person you are to marry? Genesis 2:19–24 (we are to marry a member of the opposite gender); 2 Corinthians 6:14 (we are not to be joined with unbelievers but are to marry a Christian).

Because we are all members of the same race (the human race), is there any such thing as "interracial" marriage? No. In fact, the Bible mentions those who have married others from a different people group. For example, Ruth was a Moabitess who had trusted in the true God of the Israelites. She married the Israelite Boaz and is listed in the lineage from Adam to Christ (Matthew 1:5).

The only "interracial marriage" that God says we should not enter into occurs when a child of the last Adam (one who is a new creation in Christ—a Christian) marries an unregenerate child of the first Adam (one who is dead in trespasses and sin—a non-Christian). Examples of such "mixed marriages" and their negative consequences can be seen in Nehemiah 9 and 10, and Numbers 25.

- www.answersingenesis.org/go/family.

Recommended Resources

- *All God's Children* by Ken Ham
- *One Blood: The Biblical Answer to Racism* by Ken Ham, Carl Wieland, and Don Batten
- www.answersingenesis.org/go/racism

Why do we look different?

Jesus loves the little children—all the children of the world ... Red, yellow, black and white, they are precious in His sight.

We've probably all sung this song at one time or another. But is it really true? Are there really red, yellow, black, and white children? The answer, believe it or not, is, "Not really."

Let's find out why ...

If you were to look through a microscope at a piece of your skin, you would find lots of interesting cells. Some help repair your skin when you cut it. Others help to continually make new skin to replace that which wears off at the surface. Still others (called "melanocytes") make a pigment (called "melanin") that helps to give your skin some color. The more melanin that these melanocytes produce, the darker the skin will be.

Scientists have found that we all have the same amount of melanocytes in our bodies.

Inside each melanocyte is a set of "instructions" (called DNA). The DNA tells the melanocyte how much melanin to produce, among other things. If the instructions in your body tell your melanocytes to make a lot of melanin, and your skin keeps a lot of the melanin that is made, then your skin will be very dark brown. If your instructions say "make a little melanin," then your skin will be very light brown. And there are all combinations in between.

So, no one really has "red" or "yellow" or "black" skin. We all share the same brownish pigment; our bodies just have more or less of it!

The very same pigment, melanin, also determines the color of your eyes. If you have a lot of it in the iris of your eyes, they will be brown. If you have a little melanin, your eyes will be blue. Brown and black hair results from a lot of melanin in the hair shafts, blond hair from less melanin.

Melanin consists of two forms, normally produced together. One is dark brownish, the other reddish.

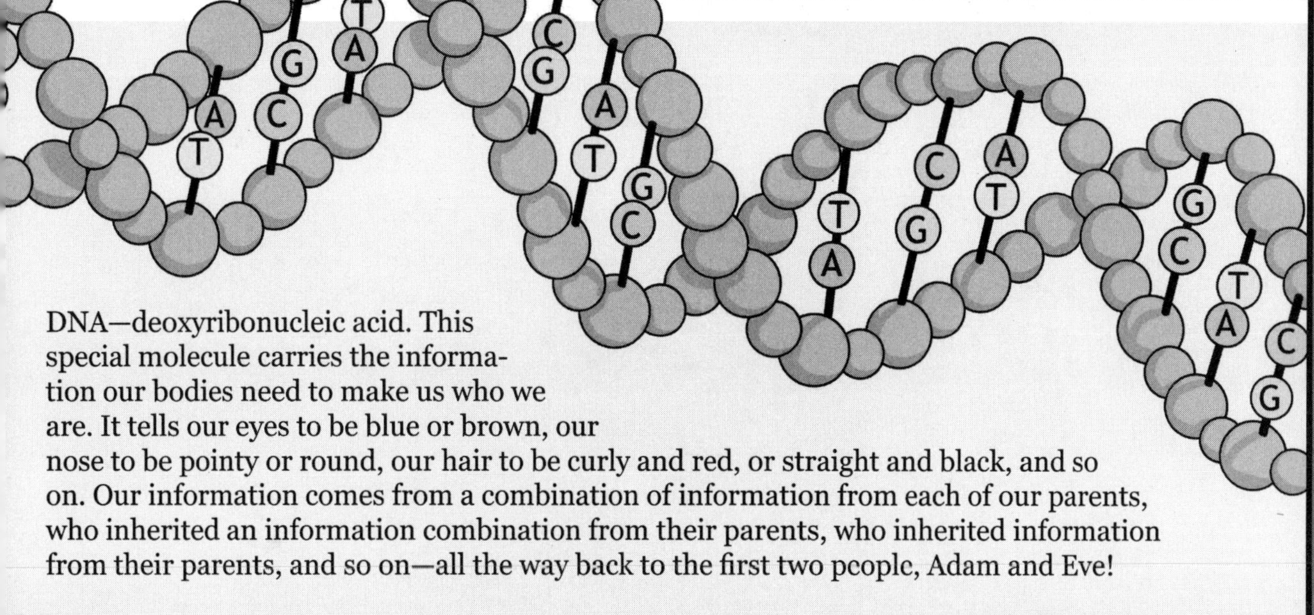

DNA—deoxyribonucleic acid. This special molecule carries the information our bodies need to make us who we are. It tells our eyes to be blue or brown, our nose to be pointy or round, our hair to be curly and red, or straight and black, and so on. Our information comes from a combination of information from each of our parents, who inherited an information combination from their parents, who inherited information from their parents, and so on—all the way back to the first two people, Adam and Eve!

People groups

Some people groups tend to have dark, curly hair with dark eyes, and dark skin. Other groups have black, straight hair, dark almond-shaped eyes, and lighter skin. Still others have light hair, blue eyes, and very fair skin.

Why? Well, it started around 4,200 years ago—at a place called Babel (probably corresponding to the later name Babylon). Noah's descendants had decided to disobey the Creator's command to spread out and fill the earth after the great Flood. They wanted to stay together; so they built a tall tower (Genesis 11:4). So, God gave to each family group a different language. This made it impossible for the groups to understand each other. So they split apart. Each extended family went its own way and found a different place to live.

As they went, each of these groups took with it its own special set of characteristics (for instance, for lighter skin and eye color, or for darker skin and eye color). These characteristics were passed through their DNA to their children, and so on. Because the groups no longer freely mixed with other groups, the characteristics of each became more and more prominent as new generations of children were born.

If we were to travel back in time to Babel, and mix up the people into completely different family groups, then people groups with completely different characteristics might result. For instance, we might find a fair-skinned group with tight, curly dark hair that has blue, almond-shaped eyes, or a group with very dark skin, blue eyes, and straight brown hair!

Even though we may speak very different languages, we are actually all part of the same family. Noah was the great, great, great, great, great, great, great, great, etc., grandfather of us all!

We're all different.

Sometimes people use the differences between us (hair color, skin color, etc.) as an excuse to do terrible things to other people: tease them, call them names, fight with them—even hurt or kill them.

Wars have been fought because of the idea that some people groups are better than others. Perhaps because their bodies aren't as hairy or their arms aren't as long. (Japanese biologists taught this in the years leading up to World War II.) One time, a man was put on display in a zoo's monkey house simply because he was a pygmy from Africa. He was thought to be "less evolved" than the zookeepers!

These terrible crimes were committed because people chose not to regard the biblical teaching that we're really all the same.

We're all the same.

We all have the same skin-coloring pigment (just more or less of it); we all have eyes, noses, mouths, and hair (well, most of us do). And the Bible teaches that we all come from the same two people (Adam and Eve—Acts 17:26). We all have the same Creator God (Acts 17:24,25).

The Bible also tells us that we all have the same problem—sin—that separates each of us from God (Romans 3:23). We therefore all have the same need for a Savior (1 Corinthians 15:3,4). The real reason we don't get along with everyone all the time is not because of our differences, but because we're all sinners.

With the parable of the Good Samaritan, Jesus taught us that we are to love our neighbors—no matter what people group they are part of (Luke 10:25–37).

We all have the same choice.

No matter what color our skin, where we live, or how we talk, we are all faced with the same choice: where we will spend eternity.

The Creator God offers the gift of spending eternity with Him to those who believe that Jesus Christ paid the penalty for their sin by dying on a cross and rising again three days later (John 3:18).

Those who refuse this gift will spend forever in a place of darkness and torment.

What will you choose?

Adam's Family Maze
Find your way through this maze and you will trace the history of the human race!
Start
ADAM & EVE
I don't know who Cain's wife was.
Adam & Eve's Sons and Daughters
Noah and Sons
People at Babel
WE ARE ALL ONE RACE OF PEOPLE!
WE ARE ALL ONE BIG FAMILY!

LESSON

3

Why are snakes so scary?

Memory verse: Romans 8:22
Materials:
From CD:
- Illustrations 3-00–3-20
- Handout L3a
- Song *Seven C's of History*

Overview

Too often, the world that we see today is understood to be the same world that God initially created. However, this is *not* the same world that Adam and Eve first lived in. Genesis 1 and 2 paint a picture of a beautiful, "very good" world in which life flourished and peace was the norm. Genesis 3 tells us what changed the original creation into the cursed world that we live in today. This lesson explores some of the effects of the Curse (Genesis 3), and offers some insights into how animals became skilled hunters, rather than the veggie-lovers that God created them to be (Genesis 1:29–30). It is vital that we teach our children the truth about the origin of death and suffering so that they do not lay the blame for our cursed world at the feet of the Creator, as so many have done in the past.

Lesson 3

Illustration 3-00. **Welcome students to class, etc.**

During this lesson series, we are learning how to answer some of the questions that Christians are asked.

Illustration 3-01. Last week wc lcarned how to answer the question: Why do we look so different? Who can tell me how to answer that question? **Briefly allow students to discuss the answer.**

Illustration 3-02. Today, we will learn how to answer another question. We'll be learning more about the second C of history—Corruption.

Illustration 3-03. How many of you like snakes? **Allow children to express their feelings about snakes (and feel free to express yours as well!). Some children may like snakes, although most will consider them scary.**

Illustration 3-04. Most people are afraid of snakes, aren't they? Why do think most people have ophidiophobia (the fear of snakes)? **Allow children to respond: because some snakes are venomous (although not all snakes are venomous), etc.**

Illustration 3-05. Today we are going to answer the question: Why are snakes (and other animals) so scary?

Illustration 3-06. Let's begin by remembering what the world was like in the very beginning. In the beginning God created the heavens and the earth in six, normal-length days. When He was finished, He said everything was .... **Allow children to say "very good."** God's original creation was perfect. It was complete and just the way God wanted it.

Illustration 3-07. God had created plants, fruits, and vegetables for all the animals and humans to eat (Genesis 1:29–30). Even animals that we think of as primarily eating meat, like this dinosaur, would have eaten only fruits and vegetables in the beginning.

Illustration 3-08. Adam and Eve would have enjoyed hanging out with dinosaurs or snakes—animals that we consider "scary." Their world was very different from the world we live in today. Snakes and spiders weren't venomous (as we see today, not all snakes and spiders are venomous), and lions weren't ferocious meat-eaters. Other animals didn't need to defend themselves from attack. **Allow children to mention other animals that are scary today or that are adept at defending themselves against attack. Remind them that in the beginning all animals were peaceful and vegetarian.**

Illustration 3-09. However, everything changed when Adam and Eve disobeyed a command the Lord had given them. Who remembers what the command was? **Allow children to respond: God had told Adam to eat from any tree in the Garden, except the Tree of the Knowledge of Good and Evil (Genesis 2:15–17).**

Illustration 3-10. Their sin (and ours) corrupted the entire creation. **Read Romans 8:22 together.**

Illustration 3-11. Let's look at two of the changes that took place. **Read Genesis 3:14, 17–18 together.** God placed a curse on the serpent, and the serpent now had to crawl on his belly and eat dust. The second change that we read about occurred in the plants: God cursed the ground and caused it to produce thorns and thistles. It was no longer an easy task for Adam to live off the produce of the ground.

This may help to explain why snakes slither on the ground (we don't know for certain that the serpent was a snake, but most people assume that it was), and why we prick our fingers on thorns when picking a rose, if we're not careful. But our question for today is "why are snakes (and other animals) so scary?"

Theologians (people who study the Bible) have several ideas about how to answer this question.

Illustration 3-12. The first idea is that the things that animals use to attack other animals today (or to defend against attacks) had different functions before Adam sinned. And over time, the features have been modified for different uses. For example, *T. rex* (and other animals) may have been used his sharp teeth to chomp on vegetables.

Illustration 3-13. Another example is found in the bat kind. Even though vampire bats drink blood today, most species of bats feed on insects or fruit. Before the Fall, the original bat kinds may have used their teeth to pierce fruit or drink nectar from plants. Over time, some of the bats have developed a taste for blood, using their sharp teeth to pierce animal skin instead of fruits. **See www.answersingenesis.org/go/vampire-bat for more information.**

Illustration 3-14. Another example is the piranha. What are piranhas known for? **Allow children to respond: they are thought to be fearsome, flesh-eating fish.** However, another fish, called the *pacu*, is a member of the piranha kind, but it primarily feeds on plants and fruit that falls from trees near the rivers. In fact, piranhas have also been observed to feed on vegetation at times. It may be that in the beginning, the original piranha kind used its teeth to bite and tear plants. Over time, some of the species of piranha have learned to use their teeth to eat other things. **See www.answersingenesis.org/go/piranha for more information.**

Illustration 3-15. And yet another example is found among the cat kind. One lioness, named "Little Tyke," refused to eat any type of meat. Instead, she enjoyed feasting on cooked grains, raw eggs, and milk. Another lioness has "adopted" several baby antelopes over the years. Rather than trying to eat them, as we might expect, this lion has tried to protect these babies from other predators. It may be that the descendants of the original cat kinds have developed a taste for foods other than fruits and veggies over the years. **See www.answersingenesis.org/go/little-tyke and www.answersingenesis.org/go/eden-echoes for more information.**

Illustration 3-16. Another idea about why animals are the way they are is that God "redesigned" many of the animals after Adam sinned and God cursed His creation. We've already seen that the serpent changed and that plants began to grow thorns. In addition, it became difficult for women to bear and raise their children (Genesis 3:16). This may have been when God changed some kinds of snakes so that their fangs would inject venom into their prey (not all snakes are venomous—many are quite harmless). Perhaps God also changed some of the features in other animals at this time.

Yet another possibility is that, because He knew that Adam would sin, God programmed the DNA of living things with information for these defense-attack structures during the original Creation Week. And then, this information was somehow "switched on" at the Fall.

So, why are snakes so scary?

Illustration 3-17. We've discussed several answers to this question. Although the Bible doesn't say for sure, the bottom line is because of Adam's sin (and yours and mine), we are no longer living in a perfect, "very good" world.

Illustration 3-18. God has placed a curse on this world.

Illustration 3-19. But there is good news! God tells us in His Word that things won't always be this way. Our Creator has promised to restore His Creation to the way it was in the very beginning. **Read Acts 3:21, Isaiah 11:6–9, and Revelation 21:4 together. Discuss what these verses teach: lambs, wolves, leopards, children, bears, calves, and snakes will all dwell together peacefully; lions will once again be plant-eaters. There will be no more death or mourning or crying or pain.**

Illustration 3-20. This future paradise is only for those whose names are written in the Lamb's Book of Life—those who have received the free gift of eternal life. **Discuss how children can know for certain that their names are**

written in the Lamb's Book of Life: Romans 3:23, 6:23, 10:9–10.

Review the memory verse for this lesson: Romans 8:22.

Discussion Questions

1. Read the "*Did you know?*" page in the student handout. What kinds of things do you see around you that remind you of a "very good" world? What kinds of things remind you that we are living in a sin-cursed world?

   Answer: Allow for individual responses.

2. In the very beginning, Adam and Eve were never sad and were never in any pain. What things today make you sad or cause you pain? What does the Bible promise to those who believe in Christ Jesus as their Lord and Savior?

   Answer: Allow for individual responses. The Bible promises that we will one day live in a place were there is no crying or pain (Revelation 21:4).

3. Read Genesis 3:17–19. How was the ground affected by Adam's sin? What things do you see today that remind you of the curse God placed on the ground?

   Answer: Thorns and thistles are part of the curse. It became difficult for Adam (and his descendants) to get food from the ground. Allow for individual responses.

Activity Ideas

1. Print L3a (one copy for each child). Have children color the earth and draw a horizontal line across the middle of the paper. On the top half of the paper, write words that describe the earth before the Fall (e.g., "very good," tearless, joyful, full of life, beautiful, peaceful, vegetarian diet). On the bottom half, write words that describe the post-Fall world (e.g., sinful, death, disease, pain, suffering, sadness, crying, carnivory, thorns, thistles).
2. Put together two news segments: a pre-Fall segment (what news stories would Adam and Eve have reported to each other in the days before they sinned?) and a post-Fall segment (what news stories would Adam and Eve have reported to each other or their children in the days and years following their sin and the subsequent curse on the creation?).
3. Visit the After Eden cartoon site (www.answersingenesis.org/go/ae-index) and use some of the After Eden cartoons to illustrate other effects of the Fall and to compare life before and after Eden. Have students illustrate their own "After Eden" cartoon.

Extension Activities

History

Ever since Adam and Eve sinned and God cursed His creation, people have tried to counteract the effects of the Curse (in temporary ways). In fact, Jesus said that those who overcame sin's curse were blessed. For example, those who try to restore peace between people are blessed (Matthew 5:9). And Jesus performed many miracles that healed people of diseases (products of the Curse), and even raised people from the dead (sin's ultimate curse)!

Louis Pasteur was a Bible-believing scientist whose work helped to (temporarily) overcome some of sin's effects. When did Pasteur live? What did he do? What did he believe about the Bible? How has his work influenced our quality of life today? Find out more at www.answersingenesis.org/go/pasteur.

Joseph Lister was another scientist whose work was anti-Curse. When did he live? What did he contribute to the field of medicine? Find out more about Joseph Lister at www.answersingenesis.org/go/lister.

Language Arts

Imagine you were Adam and Eve. Write an essay on what it might have been like to live in the Garden of Eden, when everything was perfect. What would you have seen? What would you *not* have seen? What jobs did Adam and Eve have? What jobs would they *not* have had?

Science

The Bible teaches that part of God's curse on the serpent was that it would eat dust. Is this really true? Scientists have found that snakes do, in a sense, eat dust! Find out how by researching how snakes use their Jacobson's organ.

- www.answersingenesis.org/go/snakes

Bible

Read Genesis 1:29 and Genesis 9:3. Make a meal that reflects the pre-Fall diet of Adam. Compare that to a meal from the post-Fall world. What is different? What is the same?

Recommended Resources

- *Why is Keiko Sick?* by Stacia McKeever

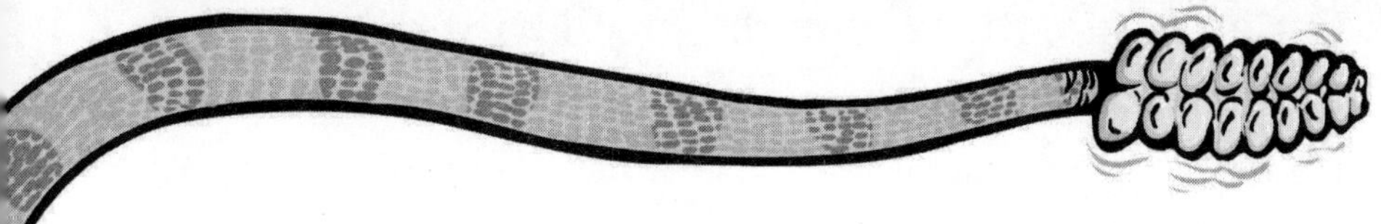

Animals with teeth!

Consider the lion ... its powerful jaws are well equipped for biting into its prey. Its stomach readily welcomes the fresh meat. But wait ... the Bible says that God gave plants to all the animals to eat in the very beginning (Genesis 1:29, 30). He declared His finished creation "very good" (Genesis 1:31). So, why does the lion appear to be so well designed to catch and digest a diet of meat? Why are snakes programmed to attack and kill animals? Why do some frogs have bright colors to warn attackers to stay away from their poison glands?

If God created everything "very good," then why do so many animals appear designed to attack other animals, or to defend themselves from attacks?

Creation Corrupted

God's perfect universe changed when

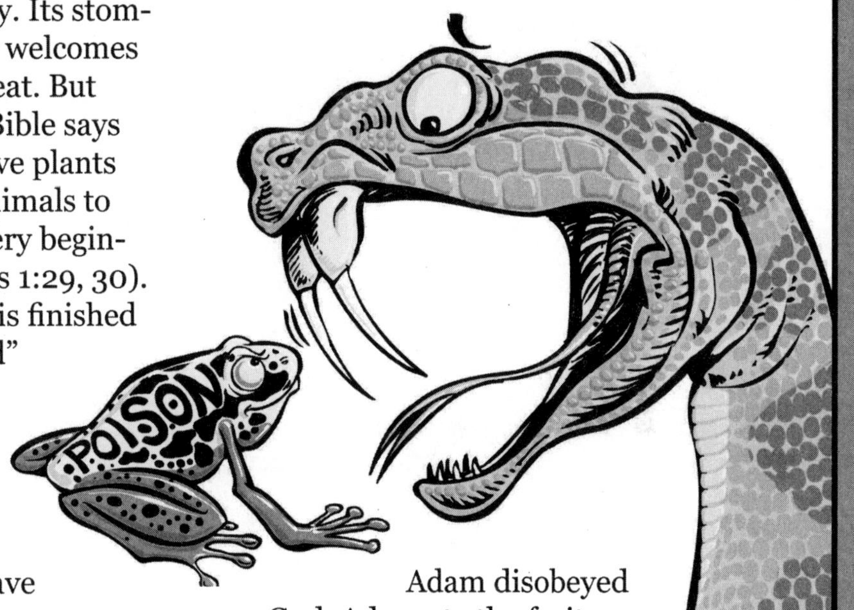

Adam disobeyed God. Adam ate the fruit from the Tree of the Knowledge of Good and Evil. This sin affected the entire creation (Romans 8:22)—including the animals.

Some Christians believe that the harmful structures (such as sharp teeth or claws) had a different function before Adam disobeyed. For example, giant pandas use their sharp teeth and claws to eat mainly bamboo. Maybe cats originally used their teeth to chomp on vegetables. Or, perhaps, the original "very good" structures have been changed by mutations over time.

Others believe that many of the plants and animals were "redesigned" after the Fall. For example, the serpent changed with the Curse God placed on it (Genesis 3:14). Thorns and thistles began to grow; so perhaps God also changed some of the features in other animals as well. Perhaps, because He foreknew the Fall, God programmed the genes with information for these structures.

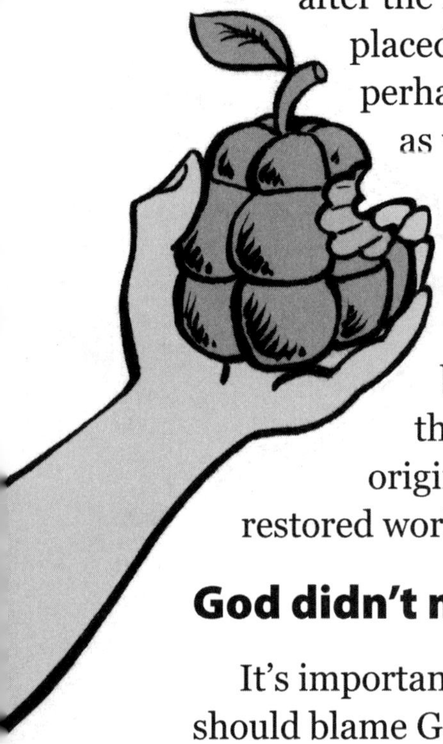

So, how did the animals change? The Bible simply doesn't give us enough information to say for sure. It may be that some of the above ideas apply for some animals, but not for others. Scripture is clear, however, that the bad things we see in today's world didn't have a place in God's original, perfect creation. They won't have a place in the future, restored world either (Acts 3:21, Isaiah 11:6–9; 65:25).

God didn't make things "bad."

It's important to remember that the bad things are not something we should blame God for. They are the result of sin—Adam's and ours (because we are descendants of Adam, and each of us sins as well). In fact, God provided a way for us to be free from the penalty of sin (eternal separation from Him). He sent Jesus Christ to die in the place of all those who receive His free gift of eternal life. And God will create a new heaven and earth. There will be no more death, pain, or other bad things.

Darwin, Death, and God

On March 2, 1841, a baby girl was born to Charles Darwin and his wife Emma. They called her Annie. Annie was their first daughter. She grew to be especially close to her father. They loved each other very much.

Tragically, little Annie became very sick. She died when she was only 10 years old. Her parents were very sad to lose their daughter. Charles became very angry and chose to blame God for her death.

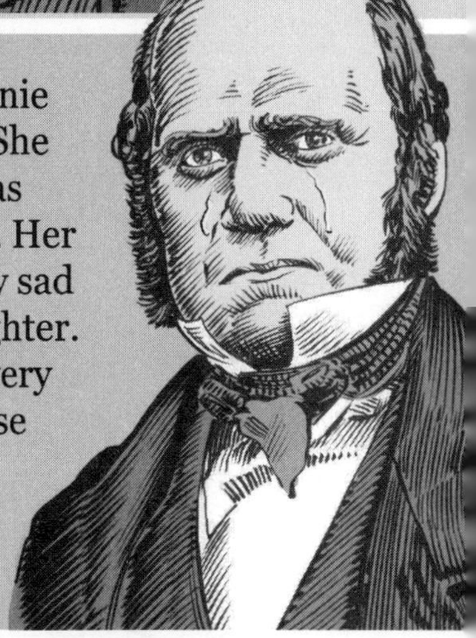

Another conflict for Charles was how could a loving, all-powerful God create animals designed to kill and eat each other? This difficulty, along with his daughter's death, caused him to reject the existence of the God of the Bible.

In 1859, just eight years after his daughter's death, Charles Darwin published a book that has caused millions of other people to reject their belief in God. This book is called *The Origin of Species*.

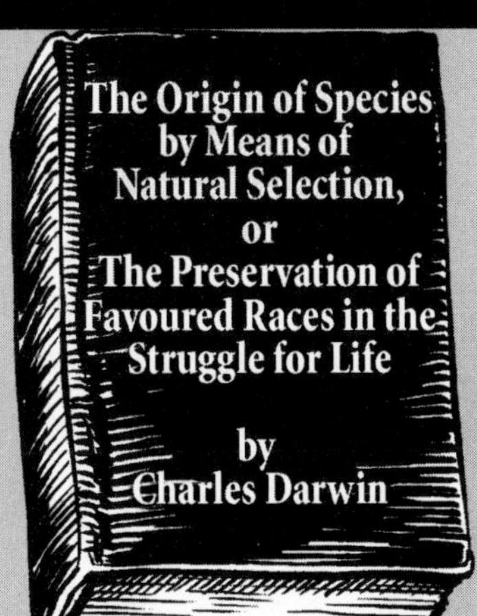

Charles Darwin didn't have a correct view of the origin of death. It's very important to understand that death isn't God's fault in that sense. Man's sin brought the curse of death. Our loving, Almighty God sent His Son to pay the price for that sin so believers could have an eternity with Him without death.

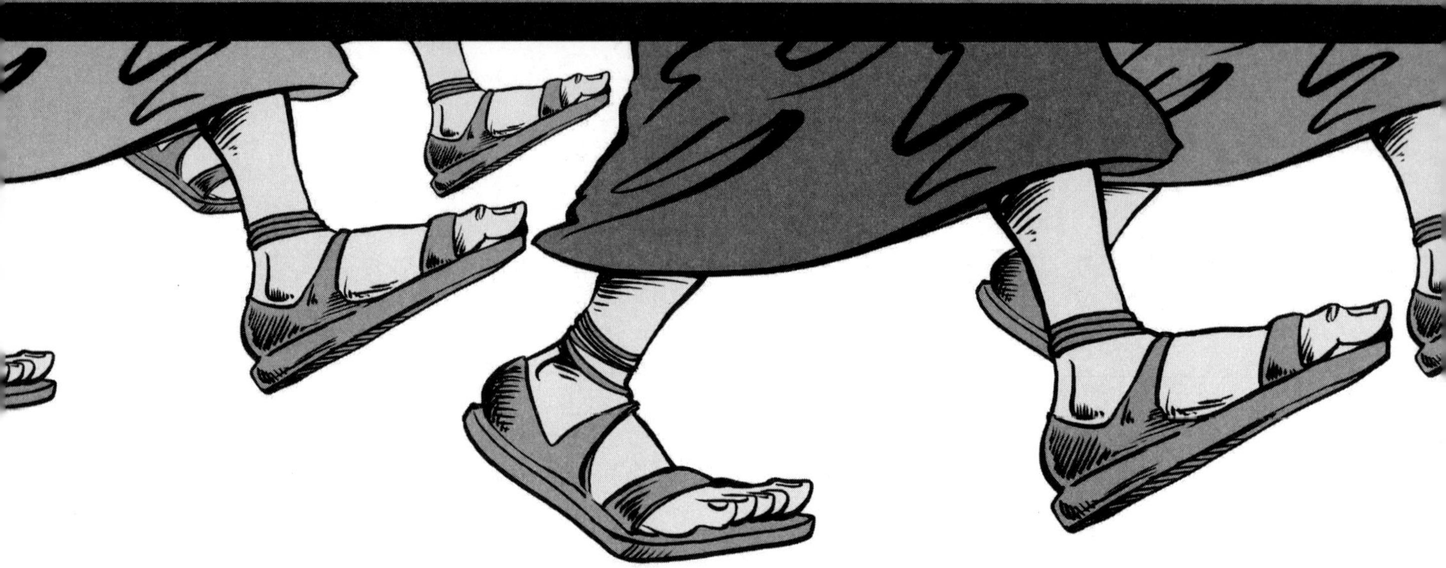

Did you know...?

Even though we are living in a world that is groaning under the weight of the curse of sin, we are still able to catch glimpses of what life may have been like before Adam disobeyed—when everything was perfect and God completely upheld His creation. For example:

- When the Israelites wandered in the desert, their feet did not swell; and their shoes did not wear out.
- When Shadrach, Meshach, and Abednego came out of the furnace, they didn't even have the smell of smoke on their clothes. They hadn't been hurt at all!
- Some types of orb-weaving spiders are able to survive for short periods of time on pollen caught in their webs, instead of on other insects.
- One lioness, Little Tyke, refused to eat any type of meat or bones throughout her lifetime. Instead she ate only mixtures of grain, milk, and eggs!

LESSON 4

Have animals evolved?

Memory verse: Psalm 150:6
Materials:
From CD:
- Illustrations 4-00–4-22
- L4a
- Song *I Don't Believe in Evolution*

Overview

Children are continually bombarded with the message that evolution is true: plants and animals have evolved over millions of year into the abundant variety that we have today. However, the Word of God relates a very different history. God created various kinds of animals to reproduce and fill the earth. Although there is great variety within each kind of animal and plant, one kind does not change into another kind. In this lesson, students will learn that molecules-to-man evolution is biblically and scientifically impossible.

ILLUSTRATION 4-00. **Welcome students to class, etc.**

During this lesson series, we are learning how to answer some of the questions that Christians are asked. **Briefly review the main points of the previous lessons.**

In today's lesson, we're going to learn how to answer the question "Have animals evolved?" How many of you have heard that over time, one kind of animal has changed into another kind? **Allow students to discuss what they've heard and what they think. Many nature programs (e.g., those on the** *National Geographic*, *Discovery Channel*, **and** *Animal Planet* **channels) and books showcase the alleged evolution of certain animals (fish, amphibians, dinosaurs, birds, whales, horses, etc.).**

ILLUSTRATION 4-01. Some people believe that life began a long time ago in a sea of chemicals that organized themselves. Evolution is the idea that over millions of years, one kind of animal turned into another kind. Eventually, the abundant variety of life we have today came about. But is this really a true story? We've already seen that humans were created in the image of God and have not evolved from apelike creatures. But what about the animals? We learned that after Adam sinned, the diet of the animals changed. But can one kind of animal really change into a completely different kind?

To find the answer, we're going to look at what the Bible and science have to say on this topic.

ILLUSTRATION 4-02. We'll start with what the Bible teaches, since God has revealed to us in His Word what happened in the beginning.

ILLUSTRATION 4-03. From the Bible, we know that God is the Creator. And that the beginning was about 6,000 years ago—not millions!

ILLUSTRATION 4-04. Let's review what God created in the beginning. On which day did God create the various kinds of plants? **Allow students to respond: Day 3. Read Genesis 1:11–13. Emphasize that God created plants according to their various kinds. This means that each kind of plant would produce more of its kind, with much variety within the kind.**

ILLUSTRATION 4-05. For example, the many varieties of cherry and plum trees that we have today are probably descendants of the same created kind. Even though they may look very different, and the fruit may taste different, these varieties of trees are in the same family, and probably share the same ancestor.

ILLUSTRATION 4-06. What did God create on Day 5?

Allow students to respond: sea and flying creatures. Read Genesis 1:20–23. Emphasize that God created sea creatures according to their kinds, and flying creatures according to their kinds. This means that each kind of flying creature would produce more like themselves, with much variety within the kind. Although we can't say for sure which of today's sea and flying creatures are descendants of the same original created kinds, scientists think that in many cases the animals grouped into the same "family" or "genus" may be members of the same kind. In many cases, members from the same kind are able to mate with each other (although the inability for different species to produce offspring in the wild or even in captivity doesn't necessarily mean they are not part of the same kind).

ILLUSTRATION 4-07. For example, there are over 1,000 species of bats, but all are probably members of the same created bat kind.

ILLUSTRATION 4-08. The various kinds of sea creatures would produce more sea creatures like themselves. For example, there are more than 350 species of sharks. Yet they are probably all descendants of the original created shark kind.

ILLUSTRATION 4-09. On Day 6, God created the various kinds of land animals. **Read Genesis 1:24–25. Emphasize that God created the various kinds of land animals to reproduce after their kinds. This means that each kind of land animal would produce more of its kind, with much variety within the kind.** The Hebrew word *min* is the word translated as *kind*. Although we can't say for sure which of today's animals are descendants of the same original created kind, scientists think that in many cases the animals grouped into the same "family" or "genus" may be members of the same kind. In many cases, members from the same kind are able to mate with each other (although the inability for different species to produce offspring doesn't necessarily mean they are not part of the same kind).

For example, the dog kind would produce a great variety of dogs, including wolves, jackals, and coyotes.

ILLUSTRATION 4-10. From studying the Bible, we also learn that two of every kind of air-breathing land animal and bird (seven of some) survived the worldwide Flood on the Ark. Many of the sea creatures were able to survive in the water.

ILLUSTRATION 4-11. These animals refilled the earth after the Flood.

Lesson 4

From the Bible, we learn that God created animals and plants after their kinds, which means that they will produce others like themselves. But the Bible does not teach that one kind can turn into a completely different kind. For example, over time a fish can't eventually turn into a frog. In fact, today we observe animals and plants reproducing according to their kinds, don't we?

Let's take a look at what scientists have discovered.

Illustration 4-12. Scientists have found that inside plants and all living things is a special large molecule called DNA (which stands for "deoxyribonucleic acid"). DNA carries the recipe that tells each plant and living thing what to look like, how to grow, and so on. Parents pass a combination of their DNA on to their children.

Illustration 4-13. To understand what this means, we'll use the dog kind as an example. Scientists have found that all dogs are descended from a wolf-type dog, which may have looked something like the one pictured here. This is probably the type of dog that was on the Ark with Noah.

Illustration 4-14. From these original dogs came many more dogs. So the dogs we have today don't look exactly like the original dogs that God created, but they are still part of the dog kind.

Illustration 4-15. As the DNA has been combined and passed down over the years, the recipe from the original dogs has produced a wide variety of dogs: dogs with short legs and small bodies (pugs), dogs with short legs and long bodies (Welsh corgis), dogs with longer legs and large bodies (deerhounds), dogs with longer legs and thin bodies (dalmatians), dogs with thicker fur (collies), dogs with longer fur (lhasa apsos).

Even though they may look very different, they are all still obviously dogs. They are all part of the dog kind. Many of the different varieties are able to mate with other varieties.

Illustration 4-16. We can use a cake mix to help explain this. From one basic recipe, we can get a variety of different desserts. We could make a large round cake, square cakes, cupcakes, a bundt cake, and so on. Even though they may look very different, they were all made using the same basic recipe. There is a limit, however, to what the cake mix and recipe can make, isn't there? Using the cake recipe and mix, could you ever make lasagna?

Allow children to respond: no, the recipe and ingredients for lasagna are different. You would have to add a lot of new information to the cake recipe, and change most of the existing recipe, as well as gain

new ingredients to make lasagna.

Illustration 4-17. Just as there is a limit to what the cake mix can produce, there is a limit to what the DNA recipe within the dog kind can produce. Dogs cannot grow fins or gills like a fish, or wings and feathers like a bird because dog DNA doesn't carry the recipe for these features.

Some people say this could happen through a series of small changes in the DNA. In fact, small changes in DNA do happen due to mutations. Mutatations are mistakes that occur in the DNA.

Sometimes, some members of a created kind are not able to survive in their environment. Natural selection is the process by which animals die out when they aren't able to adapt to their surroundings. Those members of the created kind that have the ability to adapt are able to survive and reproduce more animals like themselves.

Illustration 4-18. For example, which variety of dogs do you think would be more likely to survive in the arctic, where it's cold and snowy? Those with short, dark fur, or those with thicker, white fur? **Allow students to respond: those with thick, white fur, like the Arctic Wolf has.** Those with thick fur are able to stand the cold better, and those with white fur are able to blend in with the snow. So if a group of dogs traveled to the Arctic, those that already have thick, white fur would be more likely to survive and reproduce pups like themselves. The other varieties would die from exposure to the cold, from not being able to sneak up on their prey, or from being preyed upon by larger animals.

Which varieties of dogs would be better able to survive in hotter climates? **Those with shorter, thin fur, with colors (dark brown, tan, etc.) that enable them to blend into the grasslands, like the jackal has.**

In some cases, a new species may eventually form. However, this illustrates variation within a kind, not molecules-to-man evolution. God created the original animal kinds with much diversity in their DNA, so that as they reproduced and filled the earth, their descendants were able to adapt to many different environments. Natural selection may bring about a new species of animal, but it cannot generate a new kind of animal.

Although mutations and natural selection occur, scientists have not found a way that whole new recipes can be added by natural processes to DNA.

This is true for the other kinds of animals and plants, too. On its own, a fish could never develop the DNA recipe for lungs, legs, and arms and turn into an

Lesson 4

amphibian. A dinosaur could never turn into a bird. And a cow could never turn into a whale. Each kind will simply continue to reproduce more of its kind.

Illustrations 4-19–4-21. Let's look at a few examples of animals reproducing according to their kinds. **These illustrations show the variety within the horse kind, the chicken kind, and the ceratopsian kind (one of the 50 or so kinds of dinosaurs).**

In the beginning, God created each kind with the right mix of DNA to produce much variety within the kind. Those animals and birds that survived the Flood on the Ark were the ancestors of today's variety. Scientists have confirmed that animals reproduce according to their kinds!

Illustration 4-22. Sometimes we might hear that someone has found the fossil of a transitional form. Transitional forms are the remains of animals or plants that were supposedly in the process of transitioning, or changing, from one kind to another. In fact, if the story of evolution were true, we should expect to find thousands of transitional forms in the fossil record. However, scientists have only found a very few, and these are highly questionable fossils.

For example, some scientists say they have found fossils of "feathered dinosaurs." However, some scientists who have carefully studied the evidence have shown that, in some cases, the dinosaurs don't actually have feathers. In other cases, the "feathered dinosaurs" have turned out to be true birds! And in at least one case, the entire supposed transitional form was found to be a fake, produced by some very clever Chinese farmers (e.g., the infamous *Archaeoraptor*, see *National Geographic* 196(5):98–107, November 1999 and *National Geographic*, Forum section, March 2000).

Some of the creatures that we find in the fossil record may seem bizarre or strange to us. For example, it's not impossible that God may have programmed the DNA of some of the creatures that we call dinosaurs to produce feathers (although to-date, no dinosaur fossils with true feathers have been found). But when we hear about "transitional forms," we need to remember it is biblically and scientifically impossible for one kind of animal to turn into another kind. Instead, we can know that the creature is a descendant of one of the kinds God originally made. It's not evolving!

Review the verse for this lesson: Psalm 150:6.

Discussion Questions

1. Print some articles about evolutionary finds (e.g., from news.nationalgeographic.com/kids/index.html or www.timeforkids.com/TFK/news) and analyze them with students. Or, the previous week, assign students to bring an article which discusses an evolutionary transitional form. Which parts are fact? Which parts are storytelling?

Activity Ideas

1. The Bible mentions quite a few of God's creatures by name. A list of crafts associated with some of the animals mentioned in the Bible is available at www.dltk-bible.com/crafts-animal.htm. Choose one animal. Have students look up biblical references to this animal, and draw a picture of the animal. Discuss some of the "design features" this animal exhibits (for ideas, visit www.answersingenesis.org/go/design for ideas). Have students list some of these features on their drawing, along with the day that God created the original kind. Choose one of the craft activities about this animal for students to work on.

2. Play Bible-animals charades. Print L4a. Cut along lines. Give each child a slip of paper with the organism name and Bible reference. Have the student look up the verse and read it out loud, acting out the organism mentioned, rather than saying the name while reading the verse. Other students can guess what is being acted out.

3. Put together a "Created Kind" collage. See the Science section below for more information.

Extension Activities

History

Where did evolutionary ideas come from? Although Charles Darwin was one of the most famous evolutionists, he was not the first person to put forward ideas that molecules have turned into men over millions of years. Trace the development of evolutionary ideas over the centuries. Compile a timeline that highlights some of the major developments in evolutionary hypotheses. Find out who Edward Blyth was and his significance to this question.

- www.answersingenesis.org/go/history

Language Arts

Choose a favorite animal that you might see while visiting a zoo near you. Write your own "zoo guide" entry for this animal that is free of evolutionary and "millions of years" content. Include a picture of the animal, on which day God created its ancestors, some "fun facts," and evidence of design.

Science

Find out more about the relatively new science of baraminology—the study of the created kinds. What does the existence of ligers and zonkeys indicate?

- www.answersingenesis.org/go/kinds

In most cases, the biblical "kind" is probably not the same as what we call a "species" today. If two animals or two plants can mate and produce a truly fertilized egg, then they must belong to (i.e., have descended from) the same original created kind. For example, if the interbreeding animals are from different genera (plural of genus) within one family, it suggests that the whole family might have come from one created kind. If animals that can successfully mate are from genera in different families within the same order, it suggests that the whole order may have derived from the original created kind. However, in most cases, the kind is usually at the family level, not the order level.

On the other hand, if two species will not hybridize (mate together and produce a viable offspring), it does not necessarily prove that they are not originally from the same kind.

Try to recreate the original kinds. For more background information on this activity, visit www.answersingenesis.org/go/liger.

Tigers and lions have been known to reproduce together, producing ligers or tigons. Many believe that all of today's cats (panthers, lions, tigers, domestic, etc.) came from an original cat kind. Find pictures of all these different cats. Combine their features to come up with one idea of what that original cat kind may have looked like.

North American buffalo and cattle have produced offspring. And other types of cattle have mated together. Find pictures of the various cow types. What do you think the original "cow" kind looked like?

Donkeys and horses mate to produce mules, while other horse types (zebras and donkeys, zebras and horses) have also produced offspring. What do you think the original horse kind may have looked like?

Camels and llamas have successfully crossbred. Combine the features of llamas, camels, alpacas, guanaco, and vicuna—how do you think this "kind" looked?

Also consider an elephant kind (Asian and African elephants, mammoths, mastodons, see www.answersingenesis.org/go/riddle), a dog kind (all the varieties of dogs, including wolves, dingoes, coyotes, etc.), and a bear kind (polar, grizzly, etc.; note that pandas were probably not part of the original bear kind—they may have been a separate kind, visit www.answersingenesis.org/go/panda).

Bible

Put together a book of animals that are mentioned in the Bible. Find a picture to go with each entry. Include the biblical reference, and if appropriate, list a lesson that you can learn from the animal.

- www.christiananswers.net/dictionary/animals.html

Recommended Resources

- *Creation: Facts of Life* by Dr. Gary Parker
- *Zoo Guide* (book)
- www.answersingenesis.org/go/selection

Lesson 4

Did animals evolve?

Have you ever heard that a long time ago, fish developed arms, legs, and lungs and eventually turned into amphibians, or that birds have evolved from dinosaurs?

Some people believe that life began a long time ago in a sea of chemicals which organized themselves. Evolution is the idea that over millions of years, one kind of animal turned into another kind. Eventually, the abundant variety of life we have today came about. But is this really a true story? Can one kind of animal really turn into a completely different kind?

What does the Bible say?

The Bible teaches us that God is the Creator (Genesis 1:1). In the beginning (about 6,000 years ago—not millions!), He created plants and animals after their "kinds" (Genesis 1:11–12, 21, 24–25). This means that each kind of plant would produce plants like themselves. And the many different animal kinds would produce animals like themselves. For example, the dog kind would produce more dogs, a cat kind would produce cats, an elephant kind would produce elephants, a bear kind would produce bears, and so on. In fact, this is what we observe happening today!

From studying the Bible, we also learn that two of every kind of air-breathing land animal and bird (seven of some) survived the worldwide Flood on the Ark. Many of the sea creatures were able to survive in the water. These animals refilled the earth after the Flood.

We know that God created animals and plants to produce others like themselves. But the Bible does not teach that one kind can turn into a completely different kind. For example, a fish can't turn into a frog. In fact, today we observe animals and plants reproducing according to their kinds, don't we?

What does science say?

Scientists have found that inside plants and all living things is a special chemical called DNA (which stands for "deoxyribonucleic acid"). DNA carries the recipe that tells each plant and living thing what to look like, how to grow, and so on. Parents pass a combination of their DNA on to their children.

To understand what this means, let's use the dog kind as an example. Scientists have found that all dogs are descended from a wolf-type dog. (This is probably the type of dog that was on the Ark with Noah.)

As the DNA has been combined and passed down over the years, the recipe from the original dogs has produced a wide variety of dogs:

- dogs with short legs and small bodies (chihuahuas)
- dogs with short legs and long bodies (daschunds)
- dogs with longer legs and large bodies (mastiffs)
- dogs with longer legs and thin bodies (greyhounds)
- dogs with thicker fur (collies)
- dogs with longer fur (cocker spaniels)

Even though they may look very different, they are all still obviously dogs, and examples of the dog kind. Many of the different varieties are able to mate with other varieties.

However, there is a limit to what the DNA recipe within the dog kind can produce. Dogs cannot grow fins or gills like a fish, or wings and feathers like a bird because dog DNA doesn't carry the recipe for these features. Scientists have found that there is no known way that new recipes can be added by natural processes, for example, to the dog kind DNA.

This is true for the other kinds of animals and plants, too. On its own, a fish could never develop the DNA recipe for lungs, legs, and arms and turn into an amphibian. A dinosaur could never turn into a bird. And a cow could never turn into a whale. Each kind will simply continue to reproduce more of its kind.

In the beginning, God created each kind with the right mix of DNA to produce much variety within the kind. Those animals and birds that survived the Flood on the Ark were the ancestors of today's variety. Scientists have confirmed that animals reproduce according to their kinds, just as the Bible teaches!

Hunting for "Missing Links"

REAL ANIMALS?

Circle the real animals. Remember that one animal KIND cannot be mixed with another KIND. Example: A gorilla and a dolphin could never produce a "gorphin," but a dolphin and a small whale can produce a "wolphin."

A. JACKALOPE
Jack rabbit + deer

B. LIGER
Lion + tiger

C. ZEDONK
Zebra + donkey

D. BEEFALO
Cow + buffalo

E. LABRADOODLE
Labrador retriever + poodle

F. PEGASUS
Bird + horse

Answers: Real animals B, C, D, E
Not real animals A, F

MIX ANIMAL NAMES

Lots of animals have names that might make you think they are mixes of different kinds of animals, but they're really not.

Whenever you see an animal with a name like these examples, remember that one animal kind is not able to mix with another. God created the animals to stay within their own kind.

Can you think of more animals with names from two different kinds of animals?

Parrotfish

Dogfish

Tigershark

Bullfrog

Catbird

LESSON

5

What about the dinosaurs?

Memory verse: Job 40:15–17
Materials:
From CD:
- Illustrations 5-00–5-38
- Handouts L5a, L5b, L5c,
- Movies "Drawing Dinosaurs"
- Song *Behemoth is a Dinosaur*

Overview

Children are fascinated by the ferocious beasts featured in movies and books. Perhaps more than any other creature, dinosaurs are used to promote the idea that the earth is many millions of years old. This lesson explores a biblical view of dinosaurs and dinosaur-like creatures (e.g., swimming reptiles [plesiosaurs, etc.], and flying reptiles [pteranodons, etc.]).

Lesson 5

Illustration 5-00. **Welcome students to class, etc.**

During this series of lessons, we've been learning how to answer some questions that people ask about Christianity and the Bible. **Briefly review the content of the past lessons.**

Although we've mentioned dinosaurs in previous lessons, this week we're going to focus specifically on these creatures. Our question for today is "What about the dinosaurs?" We've probably seen quite a few movies or television programs about these amazing creatures, or read about them in books. But most of what we've heard isn't true. Let's take a look at a few examples.

Illustration 5-01. How many of you have seen or heard about the *Land Before Time* movies? One of the main themes of these movies is that dinosaurs lived and died millions of years ago—long before humans were around.

Illustration 5-02. In the movie *Dinosaur*, we learn that many dinosaurs died when a meteor struck the earth millions of years ago.

Illustration 5-03. Signs in most museums and zoos tell us that dinosaurs have evolved into birds over millions of years.

However, as we'll learn today, these things are simply *not* true.

Illustration 5-04. We've learned that the Bible is God's Word to us. It is the history book of the universe.

Illustration 5-05. We need to allow the Bible to help us understand the true history about dinosaurs, so that when we watch these movies or read books, we can tell the difference between truth and lies. We'll use the seven C's of history to guide our thinking about dinosaurs.

Illustration 5-06. Let's start with the first C—Creation. In the beginning, God created the heavens and the earth.

Illustration 5-07. How many days did God take to create everything? **Six days. He rested on the seventh.**

Illustration 5-08. On the fifth day, what kinds of animals did God create? **Discuss some of the sea and flying creatures that God created on this day (fish, octopi, sea cucumbers, bats, birds, etc.).**

Illustrations 5-09–5-10. God also created different kinds of dinosaur-like creatures on Day 5. **Technically, the different kinds of dinosaurs are animals that lived on the land, although creatures such as the**

plesiosaur and pteranodon are often considered "dinosaur-like." God said that everything He created on this day was "good" (Genesis 1:21).

Illustration 5-11. On the sixth day, what did God create? **Discuss some of the various kinds of land animals (cats, elephants, dogs, etc.), and remind students that this was the day that God created the first two humans.**

Illustrations 5-12–5-13. God also created the different dinosaur kinds, which included animals such as these on Day 6, along with the other land animals and humans. **There may have been as many as 50 different kinds of dinosaurs, e.g., ceratopsians, tyrannosaurs.**

Illustration 5-14. When God finished His creative acts, He declared that His completed creation was "very good." It was perfect and complete, and much different from our world today.

Illustration 5-15. Remember, the animals didn't eat each other. Instead, they ate the fruits and plants that God had created for them.

Illustration 5-16. We know from carefully studying the Bible that God created the heavens and the earth around 6,000 years ago. Even though some movies or books might say that dinosaurs lived and died many millions of years ago, this is simply not true.

Illustration 5-17. We've already discussed why some dinosaurs changed from eating only plants to dining on other animals for their supper.

Illustration 5-18. The second C (corruption) helps to explain this. Who can tell me what happened? **Allow students to briefly review the affects of Adam and Eve's disobedience to the command of God.**

Illustration 5-19. Adam and Eve's children and grandchildren continued to disobey their Creator, and after many years, God judged their sinfulness by destroying the earth with water—this global Flood was a catastrophe!

Illustration 5-20. God chose Noah to build an ark which would carry Noah's family and representatives of the (land-dwelling, air-breathing) animal and bird kinds safely through the earth-covering Flood. Since dinosaurs are classified as "land animals," the various dinosaur kinds were represented on the Ark. The flying reptile kinds were also on the Ark.

Illustration 5-21. Some people claim that dinosaurs were too big to fit on the Ark. However, the Ark was quite large. It had plenty of space for all the animals, plus their food and water.

Lesson 5

ILLUSTRATION 5-22. Additionally, although older dinosaurs were quite large, God probably brought younger, smaller dinosaurs onto the Ark.

ILLUSTRATION 5-23. Those dinosaurs and others animals that were not on the Ark were caught up in the floodwaters that covered the earth as a result of rain and the fountains of the great deep breaking up.

ILLUSTRATIONS 5-24–5-25. Many dinosaurs tried to escape the rising floodwaters by running to higher ground. They left behind many tracks that show their attempt to escape the water. Some even laid eggs just before the floodwaters reached their area. However, there was no escape for the dinosaurs or any of the other animals that were not on the Ark. Eventually, the water buried the dinosaurs in mud, and covered their trackways and eggs with layers of sediments. Even the highest hills were covered. In recent years, scientists have discovered some of the bones, tracks, and eggs of those dinosaurs that didn't survive the Flood. **For more information on dinosaur footprints, see www.answersingenesis.org/go/trackways.**

Remember, these fossils are not millions of years old, as you might have heard. They are around 4,300 years old, at the most. In fact, scientists have found something that confirms the bones can't be millions of years old. They found that some of the dinosaur bones were not completely fossilized and that the bones still contained what appears to be preserved soft tissue. Scientific tests have shown that this soft tissue couldn't have lasted for millions of years! **For more information, see www.answersingenesis.org/go/soft-tissue.**

ILLUSTRATION 5-26. About a year after Noah and his family entered the Ark, the floodwaters began to go down. Finally, the Ark landed in the mountains of Ararat. God told Noah and his family and the animals to get off the Ark and to spread out and fill the earth. God promised to never again flood the entire earth with water. The rainbows we see today remind us of this covenant (promise).

ILLUSTRATION 5-27. Many of the people groups that spread out over the earth after God confused their language at Babel have stories that describe their encounters with the animals we call dinosaurs or dinosaur-like today. However, they called the creatures names like "dragon," "thunderbird," "behemoth," and "leviathan," instead of "dinosaur." In fact, a man named Job recorded his experience with a behemoth for us in the Bible.

Read Job 40:15–24 together. How does the Bible describe behemoth's tail? **It has a tail like a cedar tree.**

ILLUSTRATION 5-28. This is a picture of a cedar tree. Do you see how large it is?

Illustration 5-29. Some people claim that the behemoth Job mentions was merely an elephant or a hippopotamus. However, neither of these animals has a tail like a cedar tree. Dinosaurs such as an *Apatosaurus* do!

Illustration 5-30. Job also describes an animal he calls "leviathan." **If you have time, read Job 41.** The description of this creature that Job gives is similar to the dinosaur-like sea animal we call *Kronosaurus*.

Illustrations 5-31–5-32. Other people groups also have their own accounts of encounters with what may be dinosaurs. For example, the Australian Aborigines have described a creature they call the "bunyip." This may refer to what we call the *Edmontosaurus*.

Illustration 5-33. The Chinese people also have many tales about dragons. Such stories are found around the world.

Illustrations 5-34–5-35. Other groups of people drew pictures of the animals they saw. For example, one group of people drew a picture of an animal that looks similar to a dinosaur, while another group drew a picture of an animal that looks similar to a flying reptile like a pteranodon.

So if the dinosaurs survived the Flood and at one time lived with people, why aren't there any around today? People have different ideas of what happened to the dinosaurs.

Some people believe that some dinosaurs eventually turned into birds.

Illustration 5-36. However, we know that this simply isn't true for a number of reasons. First, God created birds on Day 5—a day *before* He created the dinosaurs. Scientists have also found that there are differences in the lung structure of dinosaurs and birds, and differences between scales and feathers. If you hear that dinosaurs have evolved into birds, you know the truth: dinosaurs have always been dinosaurs, and bird have always been birds.

Illustration 5-37. Some people believe that dinosaurs disappeared when a giant asteroid hit the earth. In fact, the movie *Dinosaur* presents this idea. However, there are many scientific problems with this idea. **For more information, see www.answersingenesis.org/go/dinosaurs.**

Illustration 5-38. The simple reason that the dinosaurs are no longer around is that they died. In fact, extinction events continue today. Some scientists have estimated that several species go extinct every day. There are several reasons that dinosaurs (and animals today) may have died out over time. These include that humans continued to hunt and kill them, their habitat changed and they were unable to adjust to changes, and their source of food became scarce.

It can be fun to watch movies or read books about dinosaurs, but we need to think carefully about what we are learning, and we need to have the Bible as the foundation for our thinking about everything, even about dinosaurs!

Review today's memory verses: Job 40:15–17.

Discussion Questions

1. Dinosaurs are "missionary lizards." What do you think is meant by the term "missionary lizards"? How can you use dinosaurs as a witnessing tool to your friends or neighbors?

   Answer: The term "missionary lizards" refers to using the topic of dinosaurs as a witnessing tool. We can use dinosaurs as a way to engage people in conversation and to present the gospel to them. We can do this by showing people that the Bible actually explains dinosaurs and makes sense of the evidence we find around the world. When discussing dinosaurs, we can talk about death (after all, dinosaur fossils are dead!), and why death came into the world (because of Adam's sin). This can lead into a discussion of the gospel.

   We can also talk about the Flood of Noah's day in relation to dinosaurs: the Flood buried billions of creatures including dinosaurs, and thus is the main cause of most dinosaur fossils. And when discussing the Flood, the vital matter of salvation can also be covered: Noah's Ark is a picture of salvation in Christ, and just as Noah had to go through a doorway to be saved, so each one of us must go through a doorway—the Lord Jesus Christ (John 10:9).

   Allow students to discuss some ways they can use dinosaurs to share the gospel with others (for example, passing out "dinosaurs cards," available from www.answersbookstore.com).

2. How do we know that dinosaurs lived with people?

   Answer: God created land animals on the same day that He created people (Day 6). As land animals, dinosaurs were part of those creatures that God created on Day 6, alongside of man. Additionally, the many dragon legends and cave drawings seem to confirm that dinosaurs were contemporaries of humans.

3. When you see in a movie or read in a book about dinosaurs dying out millions of years ago, or changing into birds, how can you respond?

Answer: Allow for individual responses. We can know these things aren't true, based on what the Bible teaches.

Activity Ideas

1. Print L5a and make copies for children to color.
2. Use the movies on the CD (or your own artistic ability!) to help children draw a dinosaur, swimming reptile, or flying reptile.
3. Sculpt a dinosaur head. Molds for this activity can be purchased from www.answersbookstore.com (one mold/child). Use clay or play-dough to cover the head and a marble for the eye. Press the end of a straw into the clay to create texture on the dinosaur "skin."
4. Bake and decorate dinosaur cookies, using the cookie-type of your choice. Arrange a dozen cookies on a paper plate decorated with non-toxic markers or crayons and cover with colored plastic wrap. Include a dinosaur card (available from www.answersbookstore.com) and deliver the cookies to friends or neighbors.
5. Play "pin the tail on behemoth." Print, color, and then laminate L5b (you may want to enlarge this picture by-hand or on a copier). Print L5c and make copies for children to color.
6. Many people talk about the "age of the dinosaur." Read the student handout together and discuss the five real dinosaur ages.
7. Make your own Chinese dragon. See www.kidsdomain.com/craft/dragon.html for instructions.

Extension Activities

History

Find out more about some of the many dragon legends that are told around the world. Compare Chinese dragons to British dragons. What was the terror of Nerluc? What type of dragon did St. George slay? Which people group told stories of the bunyip? Which Native American tribes reported encounters with thunderbirds? What was the Piasa bird? What is the connection between dragons and the Ishtar Gate? What happened to the cooper who met with winged dragons in Lucerne, Switzerland?

In a three-ring binder, compile summaries (or copies of pages from books) of dragon legends, organized according to the country of origin. Draw a picture of each dragon based on the description given in the legend.

- webtech.kennesaw.edu/jcheek3/dragons.htm
- www.nla.gov.au/exhibitions/bunyips/
- www.answersingenesis.org/go/dragons

Language Arts

Write a short essay that describes your favorite dinosaur. How big did it grow? What was its post-Fall diet? What would you have done if you met this dinosaur while taking a walk?

Science

There are many differences between reptiles and birds. Find out how the following systems differ between the two types of creatures: respiratory, circulatory, excretory. In addition, find out how scales differ from feathers. How does embryonic development of most reptiles differ from embryonic development in most birds?

Bible

Read Job 40 and 41. Have children draw a picture of the behemoth and leviathan, based on the descriptions of these beasts in these chapters.

Recommended Resources

- *After the Flood* by Bill Cooper
- *D is for Dinosaur* by Ken Ham
- *Dinosaurs by Design* by Duane Gish
- *Dinosaurs, Genesis, and the Gospel* (DVD)
- *Dinosaurs of Eden* by Ken Ham
- *God's Dinosaurs* (activity books)
- *The Great Dinosaur Mystery Solved!* by Ken Ham
- *When Dragons' Hearts Were Good* by Buddy Davis

Dinosaur questions

Tyrannosaurs, triceratops, stegosaurs, iguanodons, velociraptors ... Dinosaurs are fascinating creatures, aren't they? But how much of what we think we know about them is actually true?

For instance, when did dinosaurs live? You might answer "millions of years ago!" Did dinosaurs ever live with people? "No!" you might shout. If asked what dinosaurs ate originally? "Meat!" you'd probably say. Are dinosaurs mentioned in the Bible? "Of course not!" you might think. Did dinosaurs turn into birds? "Yes!" you might reply. But actually, all of those answers are wrong.

Let's rethink the answers to these questions, using the Bible (which tells us the true history of the universe) as the foundation for our thoughts, rather than just relying on what we've always heard or been taught.

God reveals to us through His Word that He spoke the whole of creation into existence in six actual days just a few thousand years ago. So did dinosaurs live on earth millions of years ago if the earth is only thousands of years old? No. They must have come into existence sometime during those first six days.

Can you figure out when? God created air and sea creatures on the fifth day of that first week. This includes the dinosaur-type flying creatures like *Pteranodon*, *Quetzalcoatlus*, and *Rhamphorhynchus*, and the dinosaur-like swimming creatures like *Plesiosaurus*, *Kronosaurus*, and *Liopleurodon*.

On the next day, Day 6, God created all the kinds of land-dwelling creatures—cats, dogs, giraffes, horses, bears, koalas, kangaroos—and all the kinds of dinosaurs we know and love.

Did dinosaurs ever live with people?

Yes! God also fashioned the first man, Adam, on that sixth day. *Adam* was actually the first human to discover dinosaurs! This also means that dinosaurs didn't turn into birds. Birds were formed the day before dinosaurs!

What did dinosaurs eat originally?

Genesis 1 teaches that at the end of the sixth day, God declared His completed creation "very good." He instructed Adam, Eve, and all the animals to eat from the plants and trees. So, all dinosaurs (including the mighty *T. rex*!) munched on fruits and veggies in the very beginning.

The Five Real Dinosaur "Ages"

Formed c. 4004 BC

Fallen c. 4004 BC

Flood c. 2348 BC

Faded ...

Found c. AD1800 to present

God brought dinosaurs into existence on the sixth day of the very first week in the history of the universe—about 6,000 years ago, along with other animals that make their homes on land, and with Adam and Eve. It was a perfect place in which all living things dined on the green plants God created for them.

The universe was changed when Adam disobeyed and took a bite of the fruit from the tree God had forbidden him to eat. Before that sad event, death wasn't part of God's beautiful creation. But after Adam disobeyed, he and Eve began immediately to die, and the animals began to desire other food besides the plants God had given them.

As time went on, things got so bad that God judged the wickedness He saw with an earth-covering flood. He brought two of every kind of land creature—including dinosaurs!—on board Noah's Ark. There, they were safe from the storms and waves, volcanoes, and earthquakes. Those air-breathing animals that weren't selected to go on the Ark, perished in the great Flood. Water, mud, and minerals were mixed up during this time. And the conditions were right, to turn the bones of many of these animals (and also many of the sea and air creatures) into the fossils that have since been found around the world.

After the Flood, the dinosaurs, people, and the rest of the animals left the Ark and began to refill the earth. Some of the animals found it difficult to survive in the new world. The climate in some places was much colder than before (as a result of the Ice Age that started after the Flood finished). Food sources may have been much less. People were now allowed to kill and eat animals (Genesis 9:3); so humans used them for food (and also to make clothing, weapons, jewelry, etc.). Eventually those animals became extinct. As they slowly died out over the years, men began to forget that they had ever lived with the huge creatures. All that was left of the dinosaurs were their bones and stories about them.

Over the years the stories about the colossal beasts turned into legends. These were written down in various places. The actual word "dinosaur" wasn't invented until 1841, by Sir Richard Owen who was studying bones of creatures that he thought were "terrible lizards." So we wouldn't expect those ancient accounts to mention "dinosaurs." But the descriptions of the beasts, sometimes called "dragons," certainly match creatures we call, for example, *Baryonyx* and *Cryolophosaurus*. And the Bible contains a true account of *Behemoth* (Job 40)—a beast that was probably an *Apatosaurus*. Scientists have also found Native American drawings on rock walls that look remarkably like sauropods.

Dinosaurs in the Bible?

The Bible doesn't use the actual *word* dinosaur (which was first invented in 1841). But it uses some very interesting phrases to describe creatures that sound like the could be dinosaurs! For instance, God describes a beast that is the larges of His creation. It eats grass, has strong legs and bones, and a "tail like a cedar." Of course, cedar trees are huge. They can grow up to 40 feet in diameter! So this beast was no small animal. Many people believe God may have been referring to some type of sauropod dinosaur here—perhaps a *Brachiosaurus* or *Apatosuarus*!

The Bible presents a different picture from what we usually hear, doesn't it? But since it is the written word of the Creator God, we can trust it to provide us with a true and accurate picture of history that helps us understand the world we live in.

LESSON

6

Was there an ice age?

Memory verse: Job 37:7–10
Materials:

For evaporation experiment:

- Thermos with hot water (please be careful with hot water—it can scald)
- Thermos with cold water
- Two empty 2-liter soda bottles with caps

From CD:

- Illustrations 6-00–6-21
- Song *Seven C's of History*

Overview

Was there ever a time in earth's history when it was partly covered in ice? Has there been more than one ice age? Will the earth ever experience another ice age? The secular story is that the earth has experienced at least five major ice-age periods over the past several billion years. The most recent ice age is alleged to have begun around two million years ago and ended around 10,000 years ago.

However, a proper perspective on the Ice Age comes from the pages of the Bible. The trigger for *one* Ice Age was the Flood of Noah's day and its after-effects. The Ice Age is believed to have reached its peak around 500 years after the floodwaters receded (the ice covered around 30% of the earth's surface).

The material in this lesson is based on the research of now-retired meteorologist Michael Oard. He explains these concepts in much more detail in his book *Frozen in Time*.

Lesson 6

Illustration 6-00. **Welcome students to class, etc.**

During this lesson series, we are learning how to answer some of the questions that Christians are asked. **Briefly review the main points of the previous lessons.**

Illustration 6-01. Today we're going to learn about a topic discussed in movies such as *Ice Age* and *Day After Tomorrow*. Who can tell me what that topic is? **Allow students to respond: the Ice Age. Encourage students to discuss what they have learned about the Ice Age from these movies, books, or their teachers (e.g., that there were several ice ages over many thousands of years, that early man was "primitive"). You may want to watch these movies yourself before class, in order to gain some ideas for talking points.**

As with many other movies and books, most of what they teach us is not true. Today we are going to learn the truth about the Ice Age—when it happened, what caused it, how long it lasted.

To begin, let's think about a word that we often hear when we learn about the Ice Age. The word is "prehistoric." What do you think "prehistoric" means? **Allow students to respond: it refers to a time before history was recorded or written down. Allow students to discuss what comes to mind when they hear the word "prehistoric" (e.g., saber-tooth tigers, woolly mammoths, dinosaurs, cave men).**

Illustration 6-02. When we hear about prehistoric beasts, we need to remember that God has given us a record of the history of the universe. The first words of the Bible are,"In the beginning." God created all things during those first six days. So, there really is no such thing as "pre-history." We have a record of history from the very beginning!

Illustration 6-03. In fact, the Bible gives us some clues that have helped scientists figure out that only one Ice Age occurred after the Flood, a few thousand years ago. There were not many ice ages over multiple millions of years, as you may have heard.

Illustration 6-04. We'll start with an event that we're already familiar with—the Flood of Noah's day. What happened at the beginning of the Flood? **Allow students to respond: the fountains of the great deep broke open. It began to rain.** For many months, the fountains of the great deep shot hot water from deep inside the earth into the floodwaters. Volcanoes around the world erupted, dumping hot lava into the waters. What do you think happened to the oceans? **Allow students to respond: the ocean waters heated up.**

Let's take a look at what happens to warm or hot water.

Conduct this experiment, which shows that warm water evaporates more quickly than cold water. Before class, pour hot water into a thermos and cold water into another thermos. During class, carefully pour hot water into one empty soda bottle and replace the cap. Pour cold water into another empty soda bottle and replace the cap. Watch as the hot water quickly evaporates and condenses on the inside surface of the bottle, while relatively little evaporation takes place in the cold-water bottle.

ILLUSTRATION 6-05. After the Flood much evaporation took place because the ocean waters were so warm.

ILLUSTRATION 6-06. What happens when water evaporates? **Allow students to respond: when it cools, the water vapor condenses, forming clouds. Point out the condensation on the interior of the warm-water soda bottle.**

ILLUSTRATION 6-07. Eventually, the condensation falls back to earth as precipitation. After the Flood, all the dust and debris in the air from the volcanoes kept some sunlight from reaching the surface of the earth. The air stayed cool year round. Because the weather stayed cooler, there wasn't much of a summer. What type of precipitation falls in cold air? **Allow students to respond: snow, sleet, ice.**

ILLUSTRATION 6-08. For many years after the Flood, volcanoes around the world continued to erupt. The dust and debris that the volcanoes released into the air kept the temperatures cool during the whole year in many parts of the world. This means that the snow didn't have a chance to melt. It continued to build up, until great sheets of ice, many hundreds of feet thick, covered much of the land.

ILLUSTRATION 6-09. In some areas, large walls of ice, like the wall pictured here, formed.

What do you think life would have been like for those living near the great sheets of ice during the Ice Age? **Allow students to respond.**

ILLUSTRATION 6-10. Many people during that time made their homes in caves, like the family in this illustration. Let's take a look around their cave. What do you notice about it? **Allow students to respond. Discuss the following: the fire at the entrance to the cave (used to keep warm, cook, and keep unwanted animals from entering the cave); the hands "painted" on**

the wall (a way of signing one's name to a picture—we'll talk more about this later); their clothing (made from animal skins); the spears leaning against the side of the cave (used for hunting and protection); woven basket holding berries (the cave people knew how to weave baskets and also which plants were edible and non-toxic); jewelry (we'll show a few pieces in more detail later—but the point is that they were skilled at making jewelry from objects that they found or carved); the tents in the cave (used to keep warm in the chilly dampness of the cave—more on this in the next illustration). For more information on humans during the Ice Age, see "Where was man during the Ice Age? (chapter 13 from *Frozen In Time*, available at www.answersingenesis.org/go/fit).

ILLUSTRATION 6-11. Caves tend to stay around 50 degrees Fahrenheit (10 degrees Celsius) year round. This is a bit chilly when it is already cold outside (as it was during the Ice Age—year round). So, many of those who lived in caves built tents for themselves. This helped them to stay warm while they were sleeping, and to have some privacy. This picture shows how they built their tents. They used branches to make a frame. Then they covered the frame with skins. They used rocks to hold down the edges of their tent, which keept breezes from blowing through.

ILLUSTRATION 6-12. How many of you like jewelry? Many of the people groups living during the Ice Age also enjoyed making and wearing jewelry like these necklaces. The top necklace was made with fox teeth and shells. The bottom necklace was made from carved mammoth tusks. If you were to make jewelry out of items that you found near your home, what would your jewelry be made of? **Allow students to respond. Spend a few minutes discussing how they would make jewelry. Use these ideas to make jewelry during the activity time.**

ILLUSTRATION 6-13. Some of the people groups that lived during the Ice Age used stones to make tools. The tool at the top is called a "perforator." What do you think they used this tool for? **Allow students to respond: perforators were used to punch holes in leather (then needles with sinew were threaded through the holes and used to sew clothing and other items). Perforators were also used as drills: to drill holes in wood, bone, and antler.**

The bottom tool is called a "burin." What do you think this tool was used for? **Allow students to respond: burins were razor-sharp tools made from flint. It was used as a knife and could cut any material that was**

Lesson 6

softer than it was: antlers, ivory, animal bones. It was used to make sewing needles, harpoons, spear throwers, and jewelry.

Illustration 6-14. These people also knew how to make and use musical instruments, such as this flute made from hollowed out bird bone. How many of you would know how to make such an instrument? **Allow students to respond. Discuss which instruments they might be able to make (recorder, guitar, drum, etc.)**

Illustration 6-15. These people also knew how to draw magnificent pieces of artwork on the cave walls. They made their own paint by crushing natural materials (ochre, ash from the remains of their fires, etc.) and mixing them with juices from plants, fruits, and vegetables, and with egg whites, blood, and animal fat. In this illustration, the artist is painting a picture of a woolly mammoth. He is leaving a record of a successful mammoth hunt that he and his family members went on. What kinds of things would you have drawn on the walls of your cave?

We can see that people who lived during the Ice Age were quite intelligent, can't we? They were not primitive or prehistoric. Instead, they were fully human, just as we are! In fact, one of the humans that lived during the time of the Ice Age may have left us some references to it. **Read Job 37:9–10, 38:22–23, 29–30. Note that most biblical scholars believe that Job lived sometime between the Tower of Babel (c. 2247 BC) and Abraham (c. 2000 BC)—during the middle years of the Ice Age, which peaked around 500 years (c. 1800 BC) after the Flood (c. 2348 BC) and ended around 200 years later (c. 1600 BC).**

After awhile, the volcanic activity began to die down. The dust in the atmosphere began to clear, and sunlight began reaching more parts of the earth again. This helped melt the great ice sheets. Also, the oceans had cooled down. So there wasn't as much evaporation. With less evaporation, precipitation decreased. Rain and snow didn't fall as much. The ice sheets continued to melt.

Illustration 6-16. Scientists who have studied glaciers and ice movement can tell where the ice sheets were during the Ice Age. This picture shows how much of the earth was covered with ice during the Ice Age. **Point out your area on the map—was your area covered with ice at one time?**

Illustration 6-17. As the ice melted, it left behind some clues that tell us where it was. For example, the gigantic glaciers changed V-shaped valleys into U-shaped valleys, like the ones pictured here. During the Ice Age, these valleys were filled with ice, which has since melted.

Illustration 6-18. Icebergs carried large rocks for many miles. When the ice melted, the rocks were dropped. This is why we sometimes see large boulders (such as the ones in this picture) in the middle of flat plains. These are called "glacial erratics."

Illustration 6-19. When the ice sheets moved, they pushed dirt and rocks into mounds along the sides and ends of the glaciers. These mounds are called "moraines." The debris is called "till." In this picture, the ice is now gone, and a beautiful lake has filled the area carved out by the glaciers.

Illustration 6-20. The ice also scraped the rock underneath it, leaving scratch marks, like the ones pictured here.

Illustration 6-21. The Bible helps us to understand the world around us. It also helps us figure out that there was one Ice Age that occurred just a few thousand years ago, after the Flood of Noah's day, not many ice ages over countless millions of years as some have suggested.

Review today's memory verses: Job 37:7–10.

Discussion Questions

1. Do you think there will ever be another Ice Age? Why or why not?

   Answer: Since the Flood provided the right conditions for the Ice Age to commence, and since God has promised that He will never again Flood the entire earth, we can say that there will not be another Ice Age.

2. When you see an exhibit on the Ice Age in a museum, how can you decide which parts of the exhibit are based on reality and which are simply stories about the past?

   Answer: Allow for individual responses. We need to carefully evaluate what we see in light of what the Bible teaches and not simply accept everything at face value. For example, we know that statements that mention "millions of years" or pre-history are not true. We also need to be careful of human reconstructions—sometimes they may be portrayed as prehistoric brutes who were less intelligent than we are.

Activity Ideas

1. Make Ice Age jewelry. Cut string into 18-inch segments. To prevent fraying, you may want to tape each end of the string or dip each end in glue and allow to dry. Allow children to design their own necklace using various

types of pasta (rigatoni, macaroni, elbow, etc.) in various colors and sizes.

2. Paint an Ice Age picture. Use what you can find around you to paint a picture (non-toxic berries, crushed leaves, ash, etc. mixed with water for paint; feathers, animal hair, twigs, moss, plant leaves as brushes). What story does your picture tell? Is there a special event that you want to record in picture form?

3. Make Ice Age instruments. Use objects found around you to make your own instruments, just as those who lived during the Ice Age made instruments from bird bones and other objects.

    - www.mudcat.org/kids/
    - familycrafts.about.com/od/musicalcrafts/

4. Make a woolly mammoth. Glue two brown pompoms together (the "head" should be a slightly smaller size). Cut "tusks" from off-white pipe cleaners and glue to head. Glue two google eyes to head. Glue four small corks to underside of the "body" for legs. Read the "*Mammoth Mystery!*" page from the student handout.

Extension Activities

History

A common claim made by those who reject the biblical account of history is that early man was "primitive." Read Genesis 1–7, and make a list of the accomplishments of the earliest men (e.g., they knew how to make and play musical instruments, how to work with metals, how to build a large wooden ship, how to speak, how to build cities).

Even after the Flood, when mankind was once again populating the earth, technology was still advanced. Find out more about our early ancestors with the resources listed below.

What was the Acheulean hand axe used for? Draw a picture of one.

What was life like for the people who lived in the caves at Ghar il-Kbir?

What types of technology did Cro-Magnon man have? Neanderthals?

How did the Native Americans come to populate North America?

- www.answersingenesis.org/go/history

- www.answersingenesis.org/home/area/fit/chapter13.asp
- *Puzzle of Ancient Man* by Dr. Don Chittick

Language Arts

Read *Life in the Great Ice Age*. Write a short story about what you think life may have been like during the Ice Age. What would you have seen? What was the weather like? What types of stories would you have heard from the elders in your clan? What would a typical day have been like?

Science

The Ice Age played a part in forming the massive desert areas found around the world today. How?

- www.answersingenesis.org/home/area/fit/chapter8.asp
- www.answersingenesis.org/home/area/fit/chapter3.asp

Find out more about the water cycle with the following resources.

- *Science and the Bible*, volume 2, number 12
- www.units.muohio.edu/dragonfly/water/experiment.shtml
- faldo.atmos.uiuc.edu/w_unit/LESSONS/evaporation.html
- www.school-for-champions.com/science/mpemba.htm
- www.answersingenesis.org/creation/v22/i3/drowned.asp
- ga.water.usgs.gov/edu/watercycle.html
- *Science and the Bible*, volume 2, features an experiment (number 3, "Swirling Clouds") that demonstrates God's control over the weather.

Bible

The Bible describes many different instruments. Read Genesis 4:21, and skim through the Psalms. Make a list of the different types of instruments the Bible talks about. Sometimes Scripture gives a description of the various instruments. Include this description in your list when possible.

Recommended Resources

- *Life in the Great Ice Age* by Michael Oard
- *Frozen in Time* by Michael Oard (also available online at www.answersingenesis.org/go/fit)

Was there an ice age?

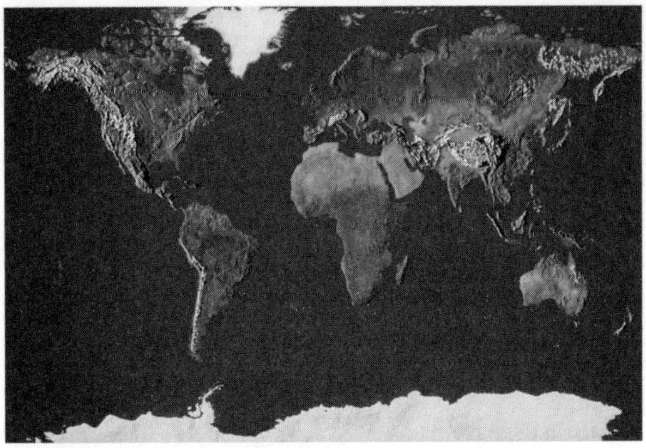

Antarctica today is almost completely covered in ice. So is much of Greenland.

But did you know that great sheets of ice used to be in many other places, like the Alps, Tasmania (Australia), and even Ohio (USA)? Where did that ice come from, and where has it gone?

Ice, ice, and more ice

Around 4,300 years ago, God judged the sin of mankind with a globe-covering watery catastrophe (Genesis 6–9). Many scientists who believe the Bible explain that this Flood provided just the right conditions for the great sheets of ice to form afterwards.

At the beginning of the Flood, the "fountains of the great deep" broke open. Hot water from inside the earth gushed into the oceans. Eventually, the land was completely covered with water.

At the end of the Flood, the waters drained off the land into the oceans. The oceans were warmer than they are today from all the volcanic activity caused by the "fountains" breaking open and the land masses moving around.

Being warmer, the water in the oceans evaporated faster than it does today. Clouds formed, like we see on the weather reports today. But these clouds were bigger. They carried more water than today's clouds, because there was more evaporation from the oceans. So, there was much more snow and rain in the years after the Flood.

Also, the snow fell over a much larger area—in places that do not have snow today. That is because the volcanoes had blasted so much fine dust high into the air that the sun's warmth was blocked from the earth. So places which are warm today were much cooler then.

The volcanic dust and clouds kept the land cool. The snow on the ground didn't melt during the summer.

Instead, it turned to ice. Gradually thick ice sheets built up. They eventually covered about one-third of the land on the earth!

After many years, the oceans cooled down. With less evaporation, there was less snowfall. Also, the volcanoes weren't as active, and the dust cleared away. The sun's warmth was able to melt the snow and ice each summer. Eventually, the "Ice Age" was over.

Altogether, the Ice Age lasted around 700 years—500 years to build up, and 200 years to melt back.

By the way ...

The Bible tells about one of the descendants of Noah (a man named Job), who possibly experienced the effects of the Ice Age. God asked Job, "From whose womb comes the ice? And the frost of heaven, who gives it birth? The waters harden like stone, And the surface of the deep is frozen" (Job 38:29–30, NKJV).

How do we know where the great ice sheets were?

Some parts of the world are still covered with ice, especially on and near the snow-capped mountains. Often the ice moves slowly down the steep slopes of the mountains. These glaciers, as they are called, grind up the rock they creep over. They carve U-shaped valleys, leave groove marks behind, and also carry heaps of broken rock long distances.

That's why we know that there must have once been much bigger ice sheets than we have today. We see the tell-tale U-shaped valleys, groove marks, and heaps of crushed rocks and boulders in many places around the world.

Although some people claim there have been many "ice ages" over millions of years, the truth is that there really was only one. It was caused by the results of the Flood. Its effects can still be seen today!

Mammoth Mystery!

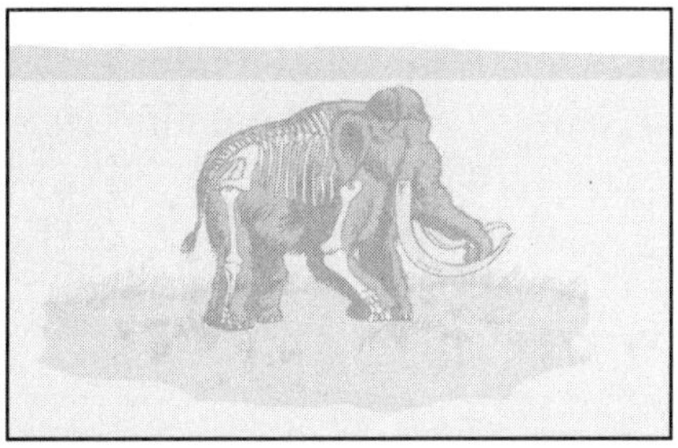

What animals come to mind when you think of the Ice Age? Ferocious saber-tooth tigers or the scary cave bear? Perhaps the most well-known Ice Age animal is the woolly mammoth, which is a type of elephant.

Where did the mammoths come from?

In the beginning, God created many different animals, according to their kinds (Genesis 1:21, 25). One of those animal kinds was an elephant kind. Many years later, Noah took members of the elephant kind (and all the other kinds of land animals!) on board the Ark with him. From these elephants have come many different elephants—the African elephant, Asian elephant, mammoth, mastodon.

After the Flood, animals moved from the mountains of Ararat to different parts of the world. Eventually, many of the woolly mammoths moved into the Siberia, Alaska, and Yukon regions. Today these areas are very cold. But during the early and middle parts of the Ice Age, these areas had warmer winters and cooler summers. It rained a lot during the early Ice Age. The mammoths (and horses, bison, woolly rhinos, and musk ox) enjoyed grazing on the grass that grew abundantly in these areas.

What happened to the mammoths?

Over time, the weather changed. It stopped raining as much as it had in the past. As the Ice Age came to an end, dust storms began blowing over the plains. The dust from these storms caused many animals to suffocate. And these storms buried many animals (including mammoths) in giant piles of dirt. Eventually, water filled the piles, and the animals became frozen in the mud and muck. Scientists have recently begun to find some of the remains of these animals.

Other animals may have drowned during the floods that happened as the ice melted. Still others may have died as the climate changed and became colder.

Mammoth Mystery SOLVED!

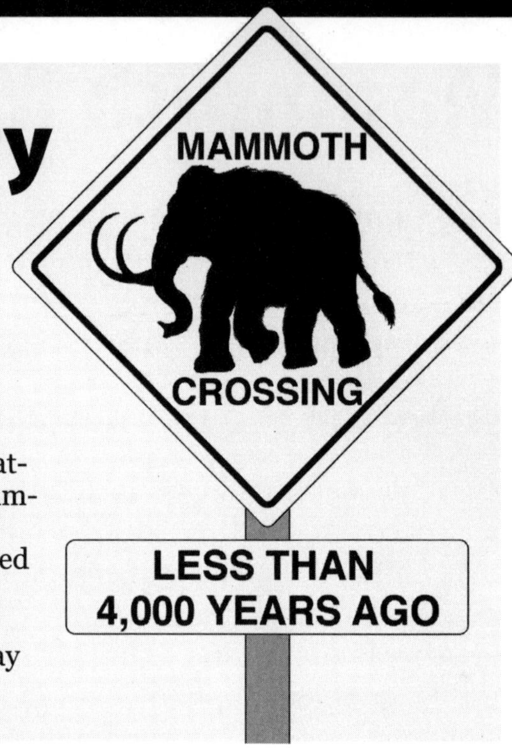

Some people believe mammoths lived and died out around 10,000 years ago. But is that really true?

By carefully studying the Bible, we learn that God created the original kinds of animals (such as the elephant/mammoth kind) around 6,000 years ago. Two of every kind of land animal (seven of some!) were on Noah's Ark and saved from the Flood, which happened around 4,300 years ago.

This means that mammoths could *not* have died out more than 10,000 years ago. In fact, some mammoths may still have been alive just a few hundred years ago!

Did you know...

- A painting of a mammoth was found on a tomb of a pharaoh who died around 3,500 years ago.
- Some elephants today have similar characteristics to mammoths: elephants in Nepal have the same sloping back, high forehead with a "dimple," and large hump on the top of their heads, like mammoths did.
- Drawings of mammoths have been found in France.
- Scientists have found drawings of mammoths in the American southwest. These pictures were done by individuals from the Anasazi Indian tribe which lived in that area from 150 BC to AD 1200.

LESSON

7 What about aliens?

Memory verse: Psalm 19:1
Materials:
From CD:
- Illustrations 7-00–7-14
- Song *I Don't Believe in Evolution*

Overview

Some of the highest-grossing movies of the past few decades are those that feature alien life forms. Even movies and television programs geared toward children are spotlighting beings from outer space (e.g., *Lilo and Stitch*). Is there really a possibility that intelligent life may exist in outer space? Should we be waiting anxiously for messages from other worlds? Are programs such as SETI (Search for Extra-Terrestrial Intelligence) and the millions of its dedicated followers on the right track?

Although the Bible does not explicitly say, "There are no intelligent life forms in other places besides earth," it *does* provide some principles that we can use to guide our thinking in this area. In this lesson, we will explore those principles, as well as the scientific evidence (or lack thereof). We will develop a biblical perspective on the topic of alien life and come to the conclusion that a galactic battle as featured in the *Star Wars* saga is very unlikely.

Lesson 7

Illustration 7-00. **Welcome students to class, etc.**

During this lesson series, we are learning how to answer some of the questions that Christians are asked. **Briefly review the main points of the previous lessons.**

Illustration 7-01. Movies such as *Star Wars*, *Lilo and Stitch*, *Men in Black*, *E.T.*, *Superman*, *Chicken Little*, and *War of the Worlds* teach us that aliens live on other planets in outer space. Some people even believe that life began in outer space.

How many of you think there may be some type of alien life out there? **Allow students to discuss briefly their thoughts about aliens.**

Some people say that there must be life out there since the universe is *so* humungous. However, the size of the universe has nothing to do with whether or not intelligent life might exist on other worlds. This isn't a good argument to use to suggest that space aliens exist.

Let's take a quick look at how big the universe is. It might be a bit difficult to really understand how big the universe is, but we'll try.

Remember, God created all the stars and galaxies that we're going to see in just *one* day, 6,000 years ago. He simply spoke them into existence. **Read Genesis 1:14–15.**

Illustrations 7-02. This illustration shows our planet earth, its position in the solar system, its position in our galaxy, and its position in the universe.

Amazing, isn't it? Let's see what else the Bible says about the heavens. **Read and discuss Psalm 19:1 (the heavens declare the glory of God) and Psalm 147:4 (God knows the number and names of the stars).**

Even though the universe is so large, God cares for His children on the one small planet we call earth. He deserves our worship. **Read and discuss Psalm 8 together.**

Illustration 7-03. Let's take a look at what we can learn from the Bible about aliens in space, and see if it's possible that Superman might actually visit us someday.

Illustration 7-04. God created the universe and everything in it in six days around 6,000 years ago. So if there *are* aliens out there, they are part of God's creation and not the products of millions of years of evolution, as some people suggest.

Illustration 7-05. However, the Bible does *not* mention space alien life forms. If extra-terrestrials *did* exist, we might expect the Bible to reveal *something* about them or tell us to expect a visit from them someday, don't you think?

Illustration 7-06. Remember, God placed a curse on the entire universe after Adam sinned. So if there *were* other beings out there, they would also be suffering from the effects of *our* sin. Does that seem fair to you? **Allow students to respond.** Additionally, when Jesus came to earth, He came as a man, didn't He? Jesus didn't become an alien. And He remains forever the God-man Jesus Christ.

Illustration 7-07. God created the sun, moon, stars, and other planets with special purposes. **Read Genesis 1:14–15 again. Discuss the purposes of the sun, moon, and other heavenly bodies. The sun gives the earth light during the day, and the moon gives the earth light during night. The stars and other heavenly bodies mark off the seasons and years and provide special signs for those on earth (remember the special light that led the wisemen to Jesus?).** God designed the heavenly bodies to support life on earth. The earth has a very special place in the universe.

What is the primary message of the Bible? **Allow students to respond.** The whole of the Bible is centered on how God has dealt with humans since the beginning. Jesus became a man and came to earth to die for the sin of mankind (1 Corinthians 15:1–4), not for a race of alien beings. He is preparing a place in Heaven for His children, not a race of extraterrestrials.

In addition, after 40 years of searching the skies for signs of life, not one real, live alien has been found, despite what you may have heard. Scientists have also found that there are many features that set the earth apart from other planets, and help us know that God created it to be inhabited (Isaiah 45:18). Let's look as some examples of these features.

Illustration 7-08. God created the sun to give us light during the day. The earth is the right distance from the sun. If it were any closer, we would burn up. If it were farther away, we would freeze.

Illustration 7-09. Because the earth is the right distance from the sun, we have liquid water. So far, earth is the only planet known to have liquid water. Over 70% of the earth's surface is covered with water! We need liquid water to live. Our bodies are made of 65% water. It helps to keep our bodies free from poisons. It helps dissolve and carry vitamins and minerals through our bodies. When we sweat, the water that evaporates from our bodies helps keep us cool when it's hot outside.

Illustration 7-10. Some have claimed that they have discovered evidence of water on Mars. To date, scientists have not discovered liquid water on Mars or any other planet. However, water in the form of ice is found throughout the solar system. In fact, some creation scientists have suggested that water in some form should be found throughout the universe, since the creation began with water (Genesis 1:1–8).

Illustration 7-11. God created our moon to give us light at night. The phases of the moon have helped people groups mark off the months and keep track of the seasons. The force of gravity between the earth and moon helps keep our oceans clean by causing high and low tides.

Illustration 7-12. Although some scientists have found other planets outside of our solar system, none of them is exactly like our planet earth.

Illustration 7-13. So, according to what the Bible and science teach us, do you think it's possible that Lilo would ever find a creature like Stitch? Or that we will be attacked by a race of alien beings? **Allow students to respond.** It seems very unlikely, based on what the Bible *does* tell us. And those who are studying the universe seem to have confirmed what the Bible says.

Instead of believing in beings who probably don't exist, we need to trust in the One who made the heavens and the earth. Who is that? **Allow students to respond: The Creator God.**

Illustration 7-14. Instead of waiting to hear a message from an intelligent life in space, we need to accept the message that our Creator has already given us in His Word. The *real* message from outer space is the message that God has given us in the Bible. Jesus Christ the Creator came to earth as a human to live a perfect life. He died and rose again so that all those who believe in Him will have eternal life.

Review today's verse: Psalm 19:1.

Discussion Questions

1. The next time you see a movie about aliens, what are some biblical principles you can think about to help you know the truth?

   Answer: The universe was created by God. It has not evolved from a big bang. The universe was cursed by God after Adam sinned. Jesus Christ came to earth to redeem mankind from the curse of sin. Jesus died and rose again on behalf of humans, not an alien race.

2. Our verse for today says the heavens declare the glory of God. In what ways can you use the heavens to tell others about our Creator?

   Answer: Allow children to respond. The size of the universe reflects the infinite nature of God. God has positioned earth the right distance from the sun and moon.

Activity Ideas

1. Make a galaxy montage using coffee filters, water-based marker, and black construction paper. Directions available at http://spaceplace.nasa.gov/en/kids/galex/art.shtml. Across the top of the montage, write "The Heavens Declare the Glory of God."
2. Several space-oriented activities with food (gingerbread robot, shuttle dog, pop rockets, cook with the sun) are featured at www.nasa.gov/audience/forkids/activities/index.html.
3. There are many ways to make a scale model of the solar system. Several examples are listed below.
   - Make a scale model of the solar system depending on the size of your sun (note, if the sun is .85 inches in diameter, you can fit the solar system into a football field): www.exploratorium.edu/ronh/solar_system/.
   - Go on a thousand-yard "planet walk" (sun is eight inches in diameter, earth is the size of a peppercorn): www.noao.edu/education/peppercorn/pcmain.html.
   - Make a toilet-paper model of the solar system: solar.physics.montana.edu/tslater/plunger/tissue.htm.
4. *Science and the Bible* (volume 3, number 13) features an experiment that demonstrates how the planets obey God's laws of motion.
5. Read through the student handout.

Extension Activities

History

H.G. Wells played an important part in developing the science-fiction genre. One of his most famous works is *War of the Worlds*. Write a short biographical sketch on Wells. Find out how evolutionary ideas influenced him, and how he, in turn, used evolutionary ideas to influence others.

- www.answersingenesis.org/go/wells
- en.wikipedia.org/wiki/H._G._Wells

Language Arts

Learn more about the science fiction genre. Who were some of its major contributors (besides H.G. Wells)? What did they believe about God? How has science fiction changed society? Choose a sci-fi work to read and analyze. Write a report summarizing your findings.

Science

1. Several Bible-believing scientists were pioneers in the field of astronomy. Choose one of the following scientists and commemorate his life on a postage stamp. On the front of the stamp, sketch important scenes from his life. On the back of the stamp, record a timeline of his life, his beliefs about God and the heavens, and his contributions to science.
    - Galileo Galilei, Johann Kepler, John Flamsteed, Charles Piazzi Smyth
    - www.answersingenesis.org/go/bios
    - Large stamp outline: www.eduplace.com/monthlytheme/pdf/stamplg.pdf
    - Small stamp outline: www.eduplace.com/monthlytheme/pdf/stampsm.pdf
2. The online NASA Kids' Club features many space-oriented games.
    - www.nasa.gov/audience/forkids/kidsclub/flash/index.html
3. Some have claimed that life originated on other planets. Is this true? Find out more at www.answersingenesis.org/go/astronomy.

Bible

1. Look up the following passages. What does the Bible say about the heavens?
    - Genesis 1:1; Genesis 1:14–18; Genesis 15:1–6; Exodus 20:11; Deuteronomy 4:19; Deuteronomy 10:14; 1 Chronicles 29:10–12; Nehemiah 9:5–6; Psalm 33:1–8; Psalm 102:24–27; Psalm 115:15–16; Psalm 121:2; Psalm 148:1–6; Isaiah 40:21–22; Isaiah 47:13–14; Isaiah 55:8–9; Jeremiah 8:1–2; Jeremiah 32:16–17; Colossians 1:13–17; Hebrews 1:10–12; 2 Peter 3:7–13; Revelation 21:1–4

- Some have claimed that the "sons of God" and/or "nephilim" mentioned in Genesis 6:2–4 are aliens. Find out more at www.answersingenesis.org/go/nephilim.

Recommended Resources

- *Taking Back Astronomy* by Jason Lisle (book)
- *Creation Astronomy: Viewing the Universe through Biblical Glasses* (DVD)
- *The Astronomy Book* by Jonathan Henry (book)
- *God's Design for Heaven and Earth: Our Universe* by Richard and Debbie Lawrence (book)
- *Destination: Moon—the Spiritual and Scientific Voyage of the Eighth Man to Walk on the Moon* by James Irwin (book)

Lesson 7

Vulcans, and Wookiees, and Spaceships … Oh my!

Superman came from the planet Krypton. Mr. Spock is from the planet Vulcan. Chewbacca is a Wookiee from Kashyyyk. Movies, television programs, and books tell us of worlds and life forms in far away galaxies.

But is any of it true? Could there really be aliens in outer space?

What can we learn from the Bible?

- God created the universe and everything in it in six days around 6,000 years ago. So if there *are* aliens out there, they are part of God's creation and not the products of millions of years of evolution.

By the word of the Lord the heavens were made, And all the host of them by the breath of His mouth. (Psalm 33:6)

However,

- The Bible does *not* mention alien life forms. If extra-terrestrials *did* exist, we might expect the Bible to reveal *something* about them, or tell us to expect a visit from them someday.
- God placed a curse on the entire universe after Adam sinned (Genesis 3, Romans 8:18–22). So if there *were* other beings out

He counts the number of the stars; He calls them all by name. (Psalm 147:4)

M80 Globular star cluster • NASA

The heavens declare the glory of God; And the firmament shows His handiwork. (Psalm 19:1)

Light Echo from Star V838 Monocerotis-December 17, 2002 • NASA

there, they would also be suffering from the effects of *our* sin.

- God created the sun, moon, stars, and other planets with special purposes (Genesis 1:14). The sun gives the earth light during the day. The moon gives the earth light during night. The stars and other heavenly bodies mark off the seasons and years, and provide special signs for those on earth. Remember the special light that led the wisemen to Jesus? The earth has a very special place in the universe. God designed the heavenly bodies to support life on earth.
- The Bible's message is about how God has dealt with humans since the beginning. Jesus became a man and came to earth to die for the sin of mankind (1 Corinthians 15:1–4)—not for a race of alien beings. He is preparing a place in heaven for His children—not for a race of extraterrestrials.

It's fascinating to learn about the heavens God created to glorify Himself and for our good. It's amazing to think that God knows the number of stars in the universe. He has given each one a name!

But, could Luke Skywalker ever bump into Yoda on Dagobah? Is there intelligent life somewhere out there on a planet far, far away? It seems very unlikely, based on what the Bible *does* tell us. And, after 100 years of searching the skies for signs of life, not one real live alien has been found!

Instead of believing in beings who probably don't exist, we need to trust in the One who made the heavens and the earth—the Creator God who offers us salvation through Jesus Christ.

The heavens are Yours, the earth also is Yours; The world and all its fullness, You have founded them. (Psalm 89:11)

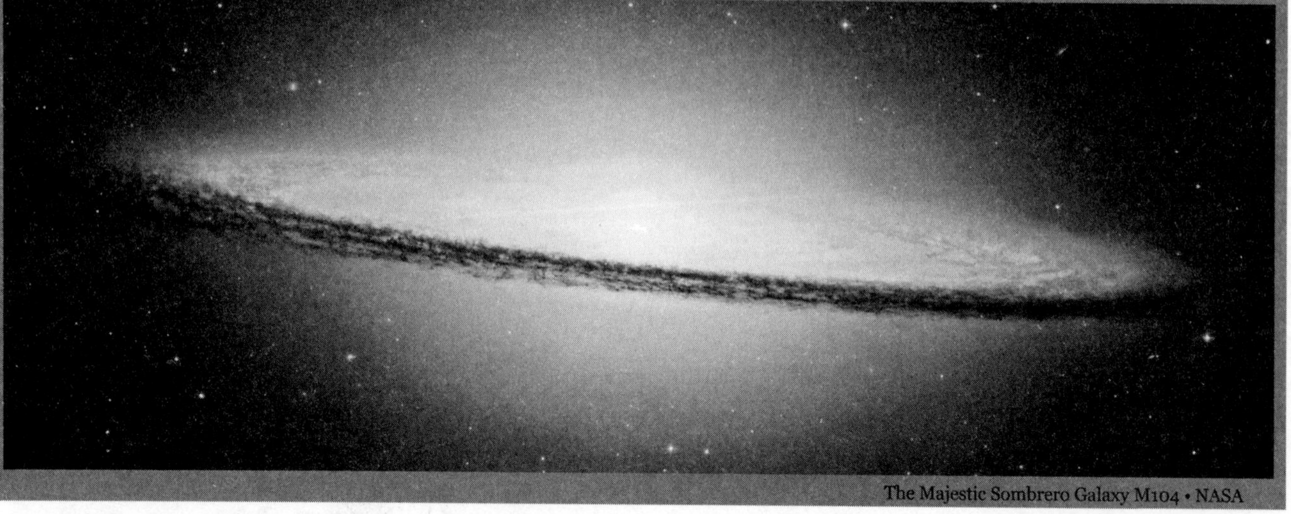

The Majestic Sombrero Galaxy M104 • NASA

ALIENS & SALVATION?

An alien takes a look at the issue of aliens!

Alien looking?

Longnose Chimaera

Many times animals that are strange-looking, such as many of the creatures that live deep in the oceans, are often described as "alien looking" meaning they look like they came from outer space. Do these creatures really look like aliens from space? How do they resemble aliens and what do space aliens look like anyway? The ideas of space alien appearance come mainly from the images we see of them in fictional TV shows and movies.

These images are produced by artists' imagination and ideas taken from creatures that live on earth. So if you think about it, even the strangest looking creatures on earth look like nothing more than earth creatures. There's nothing alien about them! Our Creator God has a wonderful and infinite imagination, and He created without using the ideas of someone else!

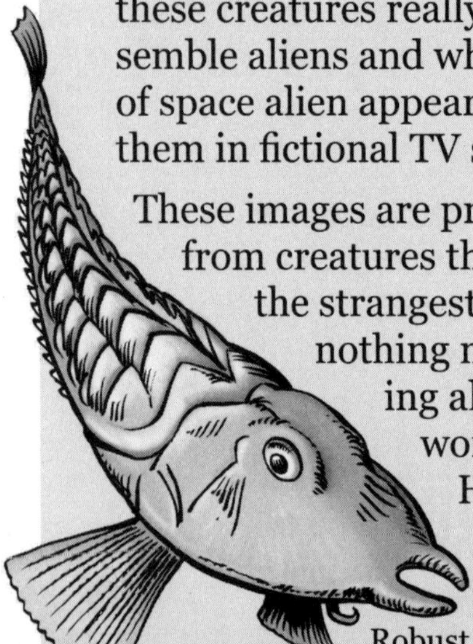

Robust armoured-gurnard

Monk

Life from beyond has visited earth!

Millions of dollars are spent each year lookin for life in outer space. But life not from earth has already visited us. Is this biblical? Solve the code puzzle below to find out.

T__e wo__ __ __e__a__e
(12; 4, 9; 7, 8, 2)

__ __e__ __, a__ __
(10, 1, 5, 12; 3, 9)

__i__e__ a__o__ __ __u__.
(1, 6, 9; 2, 3, 11, 5)

JO__ __ 1:14a
(12, 3)

Code Key

1 = L	7 = B
2 = M	8 = C
3 = N	9 = D
4 = R	10 = F
5 = S	11 = G
6 = V	12 = H

NSWER: The Word became flesh, and ved among us. John 1:14a The Bible tells s that Jesus Christ, the Creator Himself, ecame a human and lived on earth for a me so that He could die for our sins to rovide the way of salvation! Life outside his planet has already been here!